# DATE DUE

| | | | |
|---|---|---|---|
| MY 9 '97 | | | |
| SE 23 '97 | | | |
| NO 18 97 | | | |
| | | | |
| | | | |
| | | | |
| | | | |
| | | | |
| | | | |
| | | | |
| | | | |
| | | | |
| | | | |
| | | | |
| | | | |
| | | | |
| | | | |
| | | | |

# INHERIT THE ALAMO

# INHERIT
# THE
# ALAMO

**Myth and
Ritual at an
American
Shrine**

HOLLY
BEACHLEY
BREAR

**UNIVERSITY OF TEXAS PRESS    AUSTIN**

*To my parents, Charlie and Joan,*

*the Northerner and the New Englander,*

*who chose to raise their children*

*in Paris, Texas*

Copyright © 1995 by the University of Texas Press
All rights reserved
Printed in the United States of America
First edition, 1995

Requests for permission to reproduce material from this work
should be sent to Permissions, University of Texas Press, Box
7819, Austin, TX 78713-7819.

∞ The paper used in this publication meets the minimum
requirements of American National Standard for Information
Sciences—Permanence of Paper for Printed Library Materials,
ANSI Z39.48-1984.

Library of Congress Cataloging-in-Publication Data
Brear, Holly Beachley, date
    Inherit the Alamo : myth and ritual at an American shrine /
Holly Beachley Brear.—1st ed.
       p.    cm.
    Includes bibliographical references and index.
    ISBN 0-292-70824-6 (alk. paper)
    1. Alamo (San Antonio, Texas)—Folklore.  2. Alamo (San
Antonio, Texas)—History.  3. Folklore—Texas—San Antonio.
4. Symbolic anthropology—Texas—San Antonio.  5. Hispanic
Americans—Texas—San Antonio—Folklore.  6. Hispanic
Americans—Texas—San Antonio—Ethnic identity.  7. San
Antonio (Tex.)—Social life and customs.  I. Title.
GR110.T5B74  1995
398'.09764'351—dc20                              94-17220

# Contents

# ILLUSTRATIONS

# Acknowledgments

This study of the Alamo involves a delicate balancing act, both on my part as anthropologist and on the part of my informants, who must continue to live with one another after the work is published. Symbolic analysis of the Alamo, as part of the movement to bring anthropology home (that is, to use our analytical skills to examine our own society's conflicts), walks the fine line between academia and social action.

Such analysis proves particularly difficult for anthropologists raised in the region studied; they must distance common assumptions as well as release former social sympathies and political views. They must step outside of their cultural identity before analyzing it. These anthropologists become social critics, questioning "truths" received throughout life.

But when entering this critical mode, such analysts must be ever alert to vulnerable and sensitive toes. The most obvious task for anthropologists is the presenting of society, complete with people, symbols, and the accompanying tensions; a less obvious responsibility involves leaving the region they study open to anthropologists following them.

This requirement shapes the resulting ethnography at least as strongly as the outward observations, especially for studies of American society. I have had to exclude most of the interview material given me by informants, omitting most names and using paraphrases instead of quotations, to protect the informants who expressed serious concerns about being quoted directly. My great appreciation goes out to those informants who *have* granted permission for me to quote them. Secure in their positions and their comments, these individuals have allowed their words and their names to give life to this work.

Many people have helped me form and conduct this study. I am especially indebted to the following individuals and organizations who have given their time, resources, and energy to this project: Sons of the Republic of Texas (SRT) members Robert Benavides, John Leal, and Reynaldo Esparza; the Daughters of the Republic of Texas (DRT), the Alamo Mission Chapter, and the Alamo administration, particularly the late Bernice Strong, librarian in the DRT library; the Texas Cavaliers; several Rey Feos Anteriores, most especially Sonny Melendrez; San Antonio historian Henry Guerra; San Antonio Living Historians Association (SALHA) members Mike Waters, Kevin Young, Steve Hardin, and Dan Cozart; administrators in the Guadalupe Cultural Arts Center, particularly Juan Tejeda; administrators in the Institute of Texan Cultures Gerry Poyo and David Haynes; League of United Latin American Citizens (LULAC) past president Jose Garcia de Lara; faculty members of the University of Texas at San Antonio Anne Fox and Waynne Cox (archaeology) and Gilbert Hinojosa (history); Nef Garcia at St. Mary's University (political science); faculty members at the University of Texas at Austin Jose Limon (anthropology) and James Kinneavy and Don Graham (English); librarians at the Barker Texas History Center in Austin, particularly Steve Stappenbeck; the Texas Historical Commission, most especially Curtis Tunnell, Jim Steely, Mario Sanchez, and Demetrio Jimenez; Glenn Greenwood of the Texas Education Agency; anthropologist Michaele Haynes in San Antonio, who has given me a place to stay while doing field work there as well as valuable insights into Fiesta royalty; my mentors Richard Handler, Jeffrey Hantman, Fred Damon, Edward Ayers, and most especially Chuck Perdue, and his wife Nan Perdue, for their suggestions and support throughout this study; my colleagues Cindy Robins, Bruce Koplin, Sara Dell, Sandra Bamford, and Anna Lawson for valuable insights, bibliographical references, and moral support; my sister, Pam Beachley, who has provided information about the bills before the Texas Legislature and who has given me a place to stay while doing research in Austin; my mother, Joan Beachley, for help in editing and for empathy as we both have gone through the graduate school process; and Ann Brear, for being on call for my family when I was out of town.

My deepest appreciation goes to my husband, Russell Brear, who has listened to and critiqued my various presentations of this material, and to our sons, Isaac and David; they have given me financial and emotional support, and have helped me keep the whole project in perspective.

# Introduction

Our historic battlefields remain our battlegrounds. They are still where we fight the social and political Other, but with images and words rather than with guns. Here we create boundaries between "us" and "them" with identities born from historic individuals, identities inherited by entire groups in current society. Our battle sites, in being the origin of these images, become our most hallowed ground and the object of patriotic pilgrimages.

This study examines one such battle site—the Alamo in San Antonio, Texas—and the conflict of identities continuing there. Visitors to this most sacred site in Texas do not have to ask what the Alamo *means*. The brass plaque to the right of the front doors outlines the site's progression to sacred status:

> The Alamo
> San Antonio
> de Valero
> Mission
> Fortress
> Shrine
> Cradle of
> Texas Liberty

The last two titles—Shrine and Cradle of Texas Liberty—reveal the sanctifying death/rebirth scenario attached to the site: as "cradle," the Alamo, in the center of San Antonio, births Texas.

Because the Alamo is the purported origin of Texas society, claiming its past is a principal means of establishing groups and individuals as being heirs to the present. But whether or not individuals claim the battle site projected in popular press and film depends on the identity they receive there; an increasing number of Texans and Americans have little desire to "Remember the Alamo."

The Alamo, as a symbol, contains such intangible entities as "sacrifice" and "manifest destiny" which, according to the narratives surrounding the site, are not necessarily part of the Hispanic identity. In the Texas creation mythology, the sacrifice that gives life to Texas is made almost exclusively by Anglos for the birth of a nation separated from its Mexican ties. The main role of the Hispanic within this story line is that of executioner. As a symbol for the Hispanic identity, the Alamo's shrine status is, in the eyes of many politically active Hispanics, extremely negative.[1]

The tensions surrounding the Alamo narratives extend throughout the United States, for the Alamo also serves mythologically as a second birthplace for the American, who undergoes a regeneration in the sacrificial death inside the Alamo image. In the frontier mythology, the American arrives in Texas as the cultured individual able to take a wasteland and create a productive extension of the United States. Here the death of heroes, coupled with the near-miracle victory of Sam Houston's small army at San Jacinto, "proved," in the eyes of many Americans, that theirs was a destiny ordained by God.

Legendry deriving from this frontier mentality is particularly strong and anti-Hispanic in the state of Texas. Southwest historian Robert Rosenbaum points out that Texas was the first region of northern Mexico to be separated from Mexico, and this separation "occurred in a context of extreme violence." He notes that the violence, which was expressed in the Remember-the-Alamo myth, was characteristic of interactions between Anglos and Hispanics in Texas much more so than it was in California or New Mexico (Rosenbaum 1981:33). In this respect, the Alamo myth serves as an archetype of America's mythological "regeneration through violence" as the Anglos conquer the western frontier; the Alamo has emerged as the site of the supreme sacrifice necessary to birth a new society.[2]

However, the southwestern United States, and the nation as a whole, are experiencing a demographic shift toward a larger Hispanic population. The accompanying increase in the Hispanic political voice as more people of Hispanic origins register to vote has brought the Alamo image under increasing scrutiny. The more vocal Hispanics in Texas (and other parts of the nation) are demanding that they receive a more positive and prominent role in the history of San Antonio and the rest of the American Southwest.

Anger toward the popularized past, though always present in San Antonio, flared up dramatically in 1988 with the pending release of

Kieth Merrill's film *Alamo . . . The Price of Freedom*. Coverage of
the protest to the film appeared in *Time* magazine:

> Today more than half of San Antonio's 1.1 million residents are
> Hispanic, and some are up in arms about the way a new film de-
> picts the famous battle. *Alamo . . . The Price of Freedom* is to
> run in a giant-screened theater near the fort. Hispanic leaders
> claim the film demeans the role of nine Tejano (Texas-born
> Mexican) defenders in the siege.
>
> (*Time*, February 1, 1988)

The problem for Hispanics wishing a part in the past presented at
the Alamo is how to be included. How do they change an entire
mythology of the struggle between the good Anglo and the evil Hispanic portrayed in most Alamo films? How do they counter the ge-
nealogical image of the current Alamo custodians, the Daughters of
the Republic of Texas (DRT), and other groups associated with the
Alamo? How can the Tejano be a Texan when the proclaimed importance of the annual Fiesta celebration in San Antonio involves
the transforming of Tejas to Texas?

If politically active Hispanics are going to share in the power imagery of the present, they must be able to claim the past as created
and the tradition supposedly deriving from that past. Those who
control identities born at the Alamo receive ancestral ties to the
past, ownership claims to the present, and, if calls to "Remember
the Alamo" remain intact, inheritance rights to the future.

Identifying what persons or groups benefit from "remembering
the Alamo" is a main focal point of this study of the Alamo and its
role in mythically reproducing Texas. I analyze ritual and mythology surrounding the Alamo for the roles assigned historic individuals and, by extension, entire groups. Also at issue here is how
various groups in San Antonio attempt to counter the exclusivity of
some claims to the past, and how these outside groups try to establish their own claims to the site. In broader perspective, this is a
study of an American historic site and the dynamics of controlling
the past so as to ensure the future.

The struggle for control, though involving a national historic site,
does not involve, in the immediate sense, the entire population of
San Antonio. The groups cited in this study account for only a small
percentage of the population of that city. The vast majority of the
citizens in San Antonio do not grasp the significance of the past as

presented at the site; most simply do not care how the Alamo is run nor what is said during ceremonies held there. A political science professor at Saint Mary's University of San Antonio, Nef Garcia, described the apathy most of his students feel toward the Alamo as a socially charged arena:

> In my classes—whether it's in ethnic politics class or my Texas politics class—we touch upon the Alamo as part of the Texas history. And this generation of students, Hispanics included, either are not familiar [with] or they're pretty indifferent about what happened in the Alamo. . . . When you explain to them what happened at the Alamo, they take a detached view and say, "Well, Santa Anna did, I guess, what he had to do, and the people in the Alamo did what they had to do." But they don't particularly care, one way or the other.
>
> (Garcia 1989)

These students, and many other San Antonians, do not feel, in an immediate sense, the effect of the Alamo mythology on their lives and thus do not feel a need to combat the story line offered at the site.

The chosen subjects of this study, people who do understand the impact of imagery presented at the Alamo, are those who feel that they have something to lose or to gain in how the past is presented there. Ties to the Alamo are ties to the birthplace of San Antonio, Texas, and the American Southwest. Analyzing the interactions of these groups in front of the Alamo offers an understanding of why the past is such a valuable commodity, and why those who would claim the past trace their ancestry to this stone womb.

Kinship with the Alamo comes in the myth and ritual surrounding it: the myth declares heroes, and the ritual annually transforms ordinary people into their kin. Although groups call any function performed at the Alamo "ceremony"—a term that denotes confirmation (and a term that I have deferentially retained)—a few of these "ceremonies," especially those performed inside the Alamo church or during sacred times, have the transformative power of ritual. The Alamo, as site of symbolic rebirth, contains this transformative power. The current struggle at the Alamo, despite references to the past, is for the future.

# Chapter 1. Ancestors and Descendants

Recording the past is a politically charged process. Offering an un-slanted history of San Antonio for background information is extremely difficult, if not impossible. However, analyzing the tensions portrayed in the mythology and ceremonies surrounding the Alamo requires some understanding of the social and economic origins of the Alamo City.

Even dates used to denote the origin of San Antonio make a political statement. Of the two dates most frequently offered, the date of 1691 has become popular due to the 1991 centennial of Fiesta San Antonio. In 1691 Franciscan Fray Damian Massanet (sent by the Spanish government to explore the region for possible mission sites) named the river, known as Yanaguana to the Payaya Indians, the San Antonio River. The 1691 date gave a Hispanic tricentennial claim to the 1991 year, a balance to the centennial celebrations for the Battle of Flowers Parade (the purported origin of the current Fiesta San Antonio), a parade which has been a predominantly Anglo affair since its inception. Furthermore, the date 1691 allows a focus on San Antonio's beginnings which excludes the Alamo, the building now viewed by some Hispanics as the symbol of oppression by Anglos.

But the more frequently cited beginnings date for San Antonio is 1718. In this year the Spanish government founded the Mission San Antonio de Valero; its accompanying presidio formed the base for the town that became San Antonio. This mission compound is later known as the Alamo, so some historians and groups within San Antonio declare the beginning of the Alamo compound as the beginning of San Antonio.[1]

The "sister missions" to the Alamo followed close behind the founding of Mission San Antonio de Valero.[2] But as the Mission San Antonio de Valero was the first mission in the frontier area, it was the most fortresslike in appearance and function. An account in 1740 describes the compound as better able to withstand a siege than any of the presidios of the province. The image of San Antonio and the Mission San Antonio de Valero in the historical documents is one of a border outpost fortifying against one frontier threat or another.

In 1731 the Spanish government sent fifteen families from the Canary Islands to help settle San Antonio. The Canary Islanders intermarried with the natives, and the residents of this region came to be known as Tejanos, a term which now suggests "natives," in distinction from the Anglo settlers that came in the nineteenth century. These few Europeans in San Antonio were later joined by more numerous settlers from Mexico. Most historians of the period say that the recognized descendants of the Canary Islanders and government officials then formed a more powerful elite within San Antonio. They controlled the best farmland and were able with their wealth to build large stone houses near the main plaza (de la Teja and Wheat 1985:10).

Historian Alicia Tjarks writes that during the latter part of the eighteenth century San Antonio "maintained the traits of a border town"; the population fluctuated with various groups using this capital of Texas (so designated in 1772) as a rallying point (Tjarks 1974:143). Archaeologist Anne Fox feels that this border town characteristic, with the homogenization of ethnicities in the area and the region's distance from Mexico City, allowed San Antonio to be one of the places in which the revolutionary sentiments and strategies could develop (Fox 1990).

In the passing of Texas from Spanish to Mexican hands, the problem of how to populate the region remained. Historian David Weber depicts Spain as having been reluctant to open up the region to foreign immigrants, preferring to acculturate the natives and send in Spaniards to govern and to provide the natives role models. But Mexican officials chose to break with the Spanish means of populating its far northern regions; in 1824 the Mexican government passed a colonization law which guaranteed land, security, and exemption from taxes for a four-year period to foreign settlers. State-recognized immigration agents known as *empresarios* selected colonists and enforced regulations of the state. The most successful Texas *empresario* was Stephen F. Austin, who inherited his father's Spanish grant when Moses Austin died in 1821 (Weber 1982:158–164). Weber offers a description of the American population within the region shortly after the passage of the 1824 Colonization Law:

There is no way to determine the precise number of immigrants from the United States, but by 1830 it certainly surpassed 7,000. Meanwhile, the Mexican population had grown slowly to perhaps 3,000. Anglo-Americans not only outnumbered Mexicans in Texas by 1830, but assimilated poorly. . . . [A] warning came [to authorities in Mexico] from Mexico's minister in Washington that journalists in the United States wrote openly that Americans who settled in Texas would retain their ties to the United States and remain unassimilated.

(Weber 1982:166)

On April 6, 1830, a Mexican law went into effect that prohibited further immigration from the United States and rescinded all *empresario* contracts not yet completed. The law had little effect. As Weber notes, immigration continued to accelerate: "Crude estimates suggest that the number of Anglo-Americans and their slaves residing in Texas in 1834 had reached over 20,700, probably more than double the number of Americans in Texas just four years earlier" (Weber 1982:177).

According to most historians studying this period, the more the central Mexican government attempted to control the colonists in Texas, the more the colonists rebelled. In December 1835, Texas rebels took San Antonio from Gen. Martín Perfecto de Cos, setting the stage for the famous conflict at the Alamo between the Mexican army under Gen. Antonio López de Santa Anna and the Texas troops under Col. William B. Travis.

The defeat of the Mexican army at the Battle of San Jacinto on April 21, 1836, brought a new political and social authority to the region and to San Antonio. The position of *alcalde* became officially mayor and that of *regidore* became alderman. One of the few Anglos in San Antonio at the time, John Smith, was elected mayor in 1837. But at this point in San Antonio history, the Hispanic population greatly outnumbered the Anglo (most of the Anglo population still resided in the eastern part of Texas), and thus the aldermen were Hispanic (Broussard 1967:13–14).

After October 1837 when the General Land Office opened in Houston, there was a land rush by Anglo Americans, and San Antonio was a popular location because of the large amount of unallocated public lands. Historian Ray Broussard claims that fear of an invasion from Mexico helped create mistrust of all people of Mexican background (Broussard 1967:15–16).

In the early 1840s, Texans carried out an unsuccessful expedition into the New Mexico area in an attempt to open a commercial route to Santa Fe; later the Mexicans invaded Texas. Gen. Rafael Vasquez captured San Antonio in March 1842, and after declaring Texas to be once more under Mexican authority, he invited all former Mexican citizens of the region to return to their citizenship with Mexico. Vasquez also announced that the mayor of San Antonio, Juan Seguín, knew of the impending invasion and supported the Mexican cause. Broussard notes that this announcement by Vasquez seemed to be a deliberate attempt to discredit Seguín among the Texans. Although Seguín helped force Vasquez back across the Texas-Mexico border, many Texans doubted his loyalty to Texas, and Seguín ultimately joined the exodus of Spanish-speaking citizens from Texas (Broussard 1967:27).

The period spanning the decades of 1830 to 1860 is currently depicted by some historians as a time of disenfranchisement for many of the Hispanics in San Antonio. In historical accounts, the Texas Revolution hero Juan Seguín is transformed from a Texas patriot serving as a messenger from the Alamo and fighting the Mexican army at San Jacinto to a crusader for the rights of Hispanics in the region. Depending on who is writing the history, Seguín may be either a disappearing hero or an emergent advocate for Hispanic rights.

The record of political control in San Antonio during this time is offered by David Montejano:

> In 1837 . . . all but one of the forty-one candidates running for city elections were of Spanish-Mexican descent; a decade later there were only five. Between 1848 and 1866 each aldermanic council included one or two Mexican representatives; after 1866, however, even token representation was rare. . . . Through the early 1900s, the Mexican voice in city politics was symbolically represented by Anglo officials with familial ties to the Mexican upper class.
>
> (Montejano 1987:40)[3]

One major reason for the loss of political power by the Hispanics is the loss of prominent Hispanics such as Juan Seguín in the 1830s through the 1860s.

The Anglos retained the commercial center of San Antonio around the main plaza, the Alamo, and the San Antonio River. The United States Army's use of the Alamo as a quartermaster's depot maintained the military/commercial tone of this plaza. In 1855 William H. Menger built his house and brewery on Alamo Plaza, and in 1859 he opened his hotel next door to the Alamo to accommodate the growing number of visitors having business with the army depot.

In 1877 the first railroad line entered San Antonio. In histories about this era, the train brings with it the development of San Antonio. In the decade between 1870 and 1880, manufacturing establishments more than doubled in number, and farms increased from 266 to 1,136 (Everett 1961:59). The railroad's arrival marked a mass emigration from Mexico to Texas, beginning in the 1880s; expanding commercial agriculture brought a demand for cheap labor to harvest the crops as well as to work on railroad maintenance crews (McCain 1981:45). The number of Mexican-born people living in Texas rose from approximately 52,000 to some 71,000 in the decade 1890 to 1900 (Jordan 1986:394).

Historian Kenneth Walker notes three reasons many of the Mexicans migrating to Texas settled in San Antonio: it is within one hundred miles of the Mexico–United States border; the city had many Spanish-speaking people already living there; and its industries required primarily unskilled labor (Walker 1965:44).

Within the city's spatial arrangement, San Antonio during the early twentieth century had become divided into ethnically segregated neighborhoods; Anglos settled primarily on the north side, the relatively few Blacks on the east, and Hispanics on the west side. In her research of San Antonio women's occupations during the Great Depression, historian Julia Blackwelder found that, of the three groups, the Hispanics occupied the bottom rung of the social ladder. Blackwelder contends that the Anglos in San Antonio perceived no threat from the relatively small Black community, but were concerned over the large Hispanic population (Blackwelder 1984:3).

Despite the presumed social standings of the various ethnic groups during the early part of the twentieth century (i.e., that Hispanics occupied the lowest position), Blackwelder makes the following observation:

[B]lack women were understood to be permanent workers. . . .
Anglos in San Antonio assumed that blacks comprised a permanent underclass in which market labor by women would continue to be necessary and that the labor-force status of black women was consequently different from that of other women. Similar assumptions were not made about Hispanic women, who were less likely to work despite poverty and who were considered employable because of temporal conditions rather than their caste status.

(Blackwelder 1984:175)

The *assumed* "permanency" of the Black status may explain why the Hispanics were (and by some people still are) considered an "unassimilable" group of people.

According to some historians, the Hispanic people living in San Antonio before the Anglo influx had their defined social hierarchy with the Canary Islanders' descendants at the top. Black people in San Antonio had never been recognized as holding the top social position, although some mulatto officers in the Spanish military were so recognized, according to Alicia Tjarks, but registered as Spaniards to justify their positions within the system (Tjarks 1974:157). Possibly the number of Hispanics in San Antonio as well as the previous social history of the group there gave, and still gives, the Anglos anxiety, especially since Hispanics have appeared as "unassimilable" and not within a permanent lower-class status.

The divisions between Anglos and Hispanics became politically important during the 1950s when Hispanic groups in San Antonio began working to better their social and economic standings. The need to accommodate Hispanic voters received at least minimal notice in the 1950s by a San Antonio political organization called the Good Government League (GGL), a group which political historian Thomas A. Baylis calls "the political arm of the San Antonio economic and social elite" between 1955 and 1975:

> The GGL served as a highly effective instrument of elite integration in San Antonio, bringing together leading bankers, developers, manufacturers, and other businessmen with a scattering of other community leaders. . . . Responding astutely to the more successful challenges of its opponents, the GGL presented the voters with Mexican-American, black, and female candidates, along with a majority of Anglos; most were businessmen, and all agreed upon the need for economic development and growth in San Antonio.
>
> (Baylis 1983:99)

Two other historians researching the GGL, John Booth and David Johnson, say that most of the GGL council members, even the Mexican American ones, came from the affluent north side of San Antonio. The main criteria for the candidate were that he or she be socially prominent and economically powerful (Booth and Johnson 1983:23).

Baylis attributes the demise of the GGL to four main factors, among which are the differences within the business elite, particularly between the north side developers and the downtown elite, and the fragile nature of the Mexican American support of the GGL candidates. The business elite's internal arguing and the uniting of the Mexican American vote came at the same time as the rise of an urban Hispanic organization called Citizens Organized for Public Service (COPS). Some political historians of San Antonio describe COPS as drawing on the political-action school of Saul Alinsky and working for greater equity in city services for the predominantly Hispanic areas of the city.

COPS collaborated with the Catholic parishes to register voters within these areas, and the elections in 1977 brought the first city council with its majority of members from ethnic minorities. With this shift in the council, the north side of town, composed primarily of relatively wealthy Anglos, lost its hold on the capital improvements it had enjoyed under the GGL (Brischetto, Cotrell, and Stevens 1983:85, 91). In 1981, San Antonio elected Henry Cisneros as mayor, its first Hispanic mayor since 1842.

Some political analysts feel that the efforts of such groups as COPS and the League of United Latin American Citizens (LULAC) have influenced the political scenario, but not as drastically as it may appear. According to John Booth and David Johnson, the current social and political climate of San Antonio is one which incorporates the changes of the 1970s as well as the strong social, political, and economic control by the city's Anglo elites since the 1840s. What emerges from the 1970s is "a marriage of both convenience and necessity" between groups differing in ethnicity as well as wealth and social background. Business leaders, rather than being able to assume unencumbered support from the city council as they enjoyed under the GGL regime, are now in a defensive position, especially concerning development in various sections of the city (Booth and Johnson 1983:110, 113).

Development of the city was, and still is, greatly influenced by the population distribution in San Antonio. The map in Figure 1.1, taken from a study done by political analyst Tucker Gibson, shows the ethnic residency patterns in San Antonio. Gibson explains the residency patterns thus:

> The city is residentially segregated among the three major ethnic groups. The Mexican-American population is located in the central city, the southwestern quadrant, and the near northwestern part of the city. With the increased upward mobility of some Mexican-American families, there has been some diffusion of the Mexican-American population into the previously all-Anglo precincts in high-income areas. The city's black population is located primarily on the east side of the city. Some dispersion of the black population has also taken place since 1970, but this pattern does not match the shifts in residency for

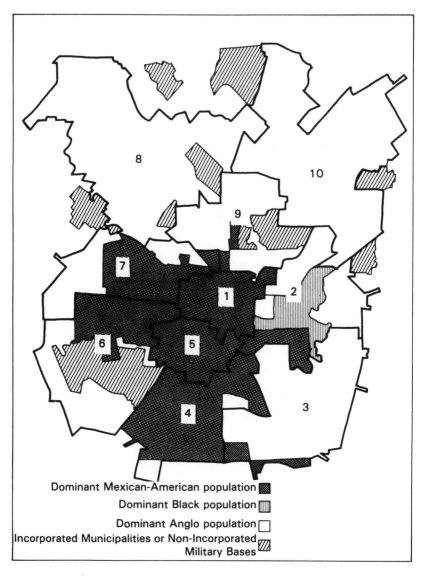

Fig. 1.1. Residency Patterns in San Antonio, Texas.
*Reprinted from* The Politics of San Antonio: Community, Progress, and Power, *edited by David J. Johnson, John A. Booth, and Richard J. Harris. By permission of the University of Nebraska Press. Copyright © 1983 by the University of Nebraska Press.*

the Mexican-American population either in terms of size or proportion.

(Gibson 1983:122)

Even with this diffusion, the Anglo population is primarily in the northern sections of the city, and the high-income Anglo communities to which Gibson refers are the incorporated townships which lie in the regions immediately to the north and northeast of the predominantly Hispanic sections. These townships are home to the majority of the "old" Anglo families of San Antonio and have been the reservoirs of status in the San Antonio community for several decades; for that reason, they become an important area for socially rising Hispanics to penetrate. They are to the immediate north-northwest of the first United States military base built in San Antonio, Fort Sam Houston (the predominantly Black section lies to the immediate south of the base).[4] In this part of San Antonio are the Argyle Club and the San Antonio Country Club, early meeting grounds for the social elite in the city. From the families living in these townships of Olmos Park, Terrell Hills, and Alamo Heights came the idea for the Battle of Flowers Parade, the purported precursor of Fiesta San Antonio.

As suggested in Gibson's designation "high-income," the per capita income in this region is significantly higher than the San Antonian median per capita income of $6,189. Table 1.1, published by the Greater San Antonio Chamber of Commerce, shows per capita incomes for the various municipalities in Bexar County. The municipalities with the lowest per capita income are to the south and to the west of downtown San Antonio and have a predominantly Hispanic population. The section of San Antonio east of Interstate 10 West and north of Interstate 10 East contains the wealthiest municipalities, including "the classic three"—Olmos Park, Terrell Hills, and Alamo Heights—which rank second, fifth, and eighth, respectively. (Interstate 10 makes an almost 90-degree angle in downtown San Antonio rather than following a straight west-to-east line.)

Booth and Johnson write that the elite San Antonians living in the classic three find themselves in a defensive position, at least in terms of the political pull they command within the city:

The old Anglo social elite, most visible in the annual rites of the Spring Fiesta and most frequently to be found at other times in the more exclusive private clubs of the city, retains an overlap-

**Table 1.1.** *Per Capita Income of Municipalities in Bexar County*

| Incorporated Cities in Bexar County | 1979 Per Capita Income | 1987 Per Capita Income | Percent Change |
|---|---|---|---|
| Alamo Heights | $13,653 | $20,521 | 50.30 |
| Balcones Heights | 8,015 | 12,452 | 55.36 |
| Castle Hills | 14,487 | 21,826 | 50.66 |
| China Grove | 6,993 | 11,740 | 67.88 |
| Converse | 5,758 | 9,540 | 65.68 |
| Elmendorf | 3,889 | 6,250 | 60.71 |
| Fair Oaks Ranch * | 22,588 | 38,766 | 71.62 |
| Grey Forest | 7,519 | 12,463 | 65.75 |
| Helotes | 9,975 | 16,478 | 65.19 |
| Hill Country Village | 18,266 | 29,974 | 64.10 |
| Hollywood Park | 12,887 | 19,787 | 53.54 |
| Kirby | 6,237 | 9,711 | 55.70 |
| Leon Valley | 8,429 | 13,042 | 54.73 |
| Live Oak | 6,343 | 9,885 | 55.84 |
| Lytle * | 6,135 | 9,560 | 55.83 |
| Olmos Park | 19,709 | 32,420 | 64.49 |
| San Antonio | 5,763 | 8,779 | 52.33 |
| Schertz * | 6,304 | 12,370 | 96.22 |
| Selma * | 6,094 | 10,053 | 64.97 |
| Shavano Park | 15,255 | 25,167 | 64.98 |
| Somerset | 5,140 | 7,683 | 49.47 |
| St. Hedwig | 7,628 | 12,592 | 65.08 |
| Terrell Hills | 16,933 | 25,124 | 48.37 |
| Universal City | 7,837 | 12,916 | 64.81 |
| Windcrest | 13,993 | 21,371 | 52.73 |
| Bexar County | 6,135 | 9,560 | 55.83% |
| Texas | 7,203 | 10,045 | 39.46% |
| United States | 7,295 | 11,923 | 63.44% |

* Cities whose incorporated area falls in more than one county
*Source:* Alamo Area Council of Government, U.S. Bureau of the Census. June 1990.
Reprinted by permission of the Greater San Antonio Chamber of Commerce.

ping relationship with the elites of economic and political power but appears to be in decline as a political force.

(Booth and Johnson 1983 : 110)

This elite's decline and the resulting position in which they find themselves in relation to the rising Hispanic society in San Antonio form a tension played out in public presentations of San Antonio's past. The ancestry claimed by each group within the city's heritage becomes the means of claiming and controlling a vital industry within the city: tourism.[5]

The other main industries in San Antonio are services and government, which, along with the retail activities of the city, provide jobs for 70 percent of San Antonio's labor force (Jones 1983:30). The industries and institutions that are moving to San Antonio are settling for the most part in the northern sections of the metropolitan area. As this is the predominantly Anglo part of San Antonio, economist Richard Jones feels that the current growth trends and the imbalances they entail will bring confrontation between ethnic groups in the future (Jones 1983:51).

The original segregation exemplified by the north and the west sides of town not only remains intact but is accentuated by the current growth patterns, despite the infiltration by wealthier Hispanics. San Antonians have not had to wait long to experience the ethnic conflict Jones foresaw in 1983. In the ongoing battle for who can claim San Antonio's past, the people living in the classic three townships on the north side of San Antonio struggle to retain their reputations as the vessels of "Culture" within the city.

Located in this part of town are many of San Antonio's "Cultural" institutions.[6] A tourist brochure produced by the San Antonio Convention and Visitors Bureau describes the various sites for the visitor to see, and for the north side of the city this brochure includes such sites as the McNay Museum ("a must for fine art lovers"), the Japanese Tea Gardens, the San Antonio Botanical Gardens, and Brackenridge Park (containing polo field, stables, clubhouse, and the San Antonio Zoo). Reservoirs of antiquated culture, which lie between fine arts and ethnicity, are located in the central part of the city: the Spanish Governor's Palace, the Navarro House, and La Villita. In the heart of town itself are the complexes intended to attract conventions to San Antonio: the Convention Center, HemisFair Plaza, and the Tower of the Americas.

Two other tourist attractions in the center of San Antonio are purportedly ethnically distinctive and are advertised as a part of the Mexican culture: El Mercado and Market Square. The former is described in the tourist brochure as "restored Mexican and Farmers Markets where open-air shopping for piñatas, pottery, and produce is still a way of life" and a "must-see for bargain hunters and Mexican food afficionados."

El Mercado and the adjacent Market Square, which are located just to the downtown side of Interstate 35, are the closest the advertised tourist attractions come to the west side of San Antonio. Here the tourists can purchase the flavor of the Hispanic community in San Antonio without entering the lower-income part of the city; this market and the more central River Walk sell ethnicity, that is, Mexican culture, within the city. In contrast, the tourist sites on the north side of town serve as reservoirs of "Culture."

In the last few years some members of the Hispanic community have attempted to declare culture with a capital *C* for their community, as well as to create a sense of community based on heritage rather than lack of income and status. The Guadalupe Cultural Arts Center is located on Guadalupe Street in the west side barrios, on the other side of the Interstate 35 thoroughfare.

But the ethnicity of the people living in the barrios of the west side is "experienced" by most tourists primarily in curio shops and restaurants in the central part of the city. Although tourists purportedly wish to experience a multicultured city, few venture into the domestic region of the majority of the Hispanic population—the west side. The undesirability of the west side is implied in the *Texas Monthly* division of the city in its guide to San Antonio; authors Nancy Foster and Ben Fairbank offer the following distinctions:

> Northwest: West of IH 10 and north of US Hwy. 90.
> North: North of Hildebrand, east of IH 10, and west of US Hwy. 281.
> Northeast: North and west of IH 35, east of Broadway as far north as Hildebrand, thereafter east of US Hwy. 281.
> Near North: The area north of the Central district bounded on the south by IH 35, on the west by IH 10, on the north by Hildebrand, and on the east by US Hwy. 281.
> Central: Generally speaking, this is the downtown area. IH 10 forms its southern and western boundaries, IH 35 is its northern boundary, while the eastern boundary is Pine Street.
> East: The East area is that part of San Antonio east of IH 35, Pine Street, and IH 37.
> South: That part of San Antonio south of US Hwy. 90 and west of IH 37.
>
> (Foster and Fairbank 1989:x)

Three divisions involve "north" as the primary distinction; there are none using "west" in that manner. Even the Guadalupe Cultural Arts Center, located *intentionally* in the barrios of the west side, is declared, by this guidebook, to be part of the northwest side of town (Foster and Fairbank 1989:233).[7]

The divisions of the city, however, meet in the center of San Antonio, which contains areas that appear either enormously Texan or undeniably Mexican. Sites in this area exhibit a "hyperreality" common in tourist attractions; the representation of the past becomes more real than the original.[8] In San Antonio, the Mexican ground in this plane of hyperreality is El Mercado and Market Square, where visitors can supposedly have Mexico in Texas.

The intensified version of the Texan culture of the north side of San Antonio appears in the center of town in the "cradle of Texas Liberty," the Alamo. The relatively small building commonly known as the Alamo is the focal point around which spreads the hyperreality. The gift shop beside this shrine of Texan culture sells tourists the symbols of the Anglos' westward movement in synthetic coonskin caps (the biggest-selling item in children's gifts), replicas of the frontier long rifle, and history books. Across the street from the shrine is the Wax Museum, in which Travis once again draws his famous line and the Alamo defenders go down fighting to the last man.[9] Adjacent to Alamo Plaza is the IMAX theater, in which actors portraying Travis, Crockett, and Bowie project their embodiment of the Texan spirit on a six-story-tall screen; here the Texas creation myth replays daily for all tourists wishing to experience, through the latest projection technology, the Alamo battle with cannon fire shaking their bodies.

Having the Alamo as "Texan" as opposed to "Mexican" or "Spanish" is extremely significant, for the Alamo is the number one tourist attraction in Texas, and it is the focal point during the most financially successful event in San Antonio's annual calendar, Fiesta San Antonio. The development of Fiesta and the current conflicts within it reveal the social climate of San Antonio, and when examined in depth, its history outlines the early and ongoing attempts to control social and ethnic imagery at the Alamo.

# Chapter 2. Fiesta Heirs

San Antonio's largest annual festival occurs during the week containing April 21, the anniversary of the 1836 San Jacinto battle between the Texas army under Sam Houston and the Mexican army led by Santa Anna. Even though Houston's victory occurred at San Jacinto, the most popular festival associated with this victory is held in San Antonio, with the Alamo as centerpiece.

The idea of an April celebration was concocted by a tourist from Chicago visiting San Antonio, but was implemented by San Antonio resident Ellen M. Slayden. Slayden organized the first Battle of Flowers Parade based on a similar flower battle she had witnessed in Spain. She cited honoring the heroes of the Alamo and the San Jacinto battle as the primary purpose of the celebration. According to the Fiesta history prepared by the Institute of Texan Cultures for the 1991 Fiesta centennial, this first flower battle and parade were so successful that San Antonians decided to hold the celebration on an annual basis. The resulting affair was known in its early years as Spring Carnival, and its activities were organized by committees of women and members of the San Antonio Country Club and the San Antonio Businessmen's Club.[1]

Arising at the end of the nineteenth century, Spring Carnival was part of a nationwide predilection for historical pageants, productions in which communities proclaimed their origins and their national role as unique. Historian David Glassberg explains that the focus of such pageants was to declare this uniqueness via historical narratives that served "both as a sacred text chronicling the nation's divine mission and as a practical guidebook of moral instruction to outline how local residents should behave in the present," based on actions of "the Founding Fathers." Glassberg notes that this focus on the past presented a local message that community leaders must be always alert to the future (i.e., development opportunities) (Glassberg 1990:11–12).

The origins of Fiesta San Antonio follow this late-nineteenth-century pattern exceedingly well. Although the Battle of Flowers supposedly commemorates the heroes of the Texas Revolution, the future of the city was certainly a concern for the people organizing the first parade. In 1891 when the idea of the Battle of Flowers surfaced, San Antonio was the largest city in Texas and was already enjoying a heavy tourist trade. The wealthy husbands of the women executing the idea were astute businessmen interested in the continuing growth of San Antonio. This focus on the tourist dollars to be reaped from such an event overrode the declared focus on the victory at San Jacinto when, in 1895, organizers moved the Battle of Flowers to June so that they could accommodate visitors in San Antonio who were attending the national convention for the Travelers' Protective Association, the largest organization of traveling businessmen.

Money and society have always been the primary ingredients for Fiesta in San Antonio. When it came time for these society women to choose a leader, they chose Elizabeth Kampmann. Local historian Jack Maguire, in his version of Fiesta's past, describes Kampmann as "an ideal choice" since she was "a descendant of one of the first families" (Maguire 1990:15). "One of the first families," as Maguire uses the phrase, certainly does not refer to the Canary Islanders, but to people arriving after Stephen F. Austin founded his colonies in Texas just before the Texas Revolution. These "first families" were Anglo, wealthy, and powerful in San Antonio business and society.[2]

In 1909 John Barron Carrington, who had moved to San Antonio at the turn of the century carrying FFV (First Family of Virginia) credentials, felt that more attention and significance should be given to the queen's image in Spring Carnival (the Battle of Flowers Parade and the events that had grown up around it). He founded an all-male organization known as the Order of the Alamo whose primary function was to select the queen for Spring Carnival. The membership for this organization was drawn primarily from the membership rolls of the San Antonio Country Club (Maguire 1990:29, 31). Such a move allowed an exclusive control by this group of men over the most visible honor for a man's unmarried daughter in San Antonio.

As the contest for social prominence heightened, the festivities of Spring Carnival continued to expand. In 1911 the primary group responsible for organizing the festival became known as the Fiesta Association, thus replacing the title Spring Carnival Association, and in 1913 the festival itself became officially Fiesta de San Jacinto. The coronation of the queen became a major event, but the role of king was still only occasionally filled. When a king did appear as part of the celebration, he would arrive in town via the train at one of the three depots.

In 1926 Carrington formed another organization, the Texas Cavaliers, who almost immediately took control of naming a king to reign during Fiesta San Jacinto. Carrington wanted the Texas Cavaliers to appear as chivalrous knights. To that end, he prescribed knightly costumes for them and organized a tourney and joust, which was held at San Pedro Park on the north side of San Antonio (near Terrell Hills, Olmos Park, and Alamo Heights). The jousts were held for two years, after which time they were abandoned, as were the cumbersome knightly costumes.

During the decade between 1920 and 1930, San Antonio's population increased by 60 percent, and Fiesta San Jacinto grew as well. The staging space for Fiesta grew with the redevelopment of the San Antonio River in the late 1930s. The San Antonio Conservation Society (SACS) began its participation in San Antonio festivals by sponsoring a fall festival on the river, known variously as Fall Festival, River Carnival, and Indian Festival. In 1948 SACS moved its festival to Fiesta week and to La Villita, calling their event A Night in Old San Antonio (NIOSA). In 1984 SACS trademarked "A Night in Old San Antonio" and "NIOSA."

As the financial success of Fiesta grew, so did the major events that it comprised. In 1948 a member of the Fiesta San Jacinto Association board, Reynolds Andricks, suggested adding a night parade to Fiesta; the resulting parade became known as Fiesta Flambeau, and it was sponsored by the Fiesta San Jacinto Association. Andricks aggressively recruited entertainment for this parade, and in 1950 decided that the parade needed its own "queen," and so created the title of Miss Fiesta. Andricks began negotiating with other cities for exchange of parade personalities' appearances, offering to send Miss Fiesta to appear in their parades if the queens of the other cities' parades would appear in the Fiesta Flambeau (Haynes 1991).

Jealousies flared. In the following decade discontent arose among organizations within the Fiesta San Jacinto Association, with some members claiming that the association, under the direction of Andricks, was emphasizing only those events sponsored by the association. Some of the most prominent organizations, such as the Texas Cavaliers, the Order of the Alamo, and the Battle of Flowers Association, left the Fiesta San Jacinto Association in protest. The chamber of commerce was called in to arbitrate the dispute, and the discontented groups rejoined when the Fiesta San Jacinto Association reorganized as the Fiesta San Antonio Commission, Inc.

The name change indicates that the jealousies revolving around Fiesta extended beyond the groups that were part of the Fiesta San Jacinto Association. Maguire notes the accompanying tensions in this management change and declares that this change "did not immediately satisfy the city's Hispanic population." Maguire also notes the lack of active participation in Fiesta by the Hispanics up to this point, saying, "With a heritage of such festivals, it is understandable why the Hispanics of San Antonio resented being only observers at Fiesta" (Maguire 1990:107). What Maguire does *not* examine—perhaps intentionally—is the change of name: the title "Fiesta San Jacinto" demands celebrating the Texan victory over Mexico at San Jacinto rather than celebrating the heritage of San Antonio itself. Maguire hints at this point when he writes, "San Antonio was, is, and likely ever shall be a 'Mexican town.' . . . Although they [Hispanics] remained silent, for the most part, there was a feeling of resentment among much of the population toward this *nuevo fiesta* [*sic*]" (Maguire 1990:106). But researchers developing the exhibit on Fiesta sponsored by the Institute of Texan Cultures declare that the name change derived from specific social and political sensitivities:

On the recommendation of the Municipal Advertising Commission the name "Fiesta San Jacinto" was changed to "Fiesta San Antonio" to promote friendship with Mexico, an action which had increased significance as plans for HemisFair unfolded. Several Hispanic organizations which had not participated before then joined the party.

(Institute of Texan Cultures exhibit for the 1991 Fiesta San Antonio)

Desire for the Fiesta spotlight apparently existed among Hispanic organizations in San Antonio's Hispanic community, but prior to this time they had not had a strong enough voice within San Antonio to question who held the controls of Fiesta imagery and personalities. Despite contributions in the first fifty years of Fiesta by such groups as the Mexican Businessmen's Association and the Mexican-American Chamber of Commerce, the royalty reigning over the festivities were all Anglo.

Due to Hispanics' growing population and increasing political voice in San Antonio, Hispanic leaders began in the 1940s to attempt some visibility for their community in Fiesta activities. In 1947 the League of United Latin American Citizens created the position of Rey Feo, a Fiesta personality based on the medieval Ugly

King crowned by peasants of southern Europe to mock their established royalty. The LULAC Rey Feo won his crown by raising the most money for the LULAC scholarship fund. This road to royalty makes the Rey Feo, according to some LULAC members, more productive and more popular (i.e., elected by the people rather than a closed organization) than King Antonio.[3]

The major participants of Fiesta now attempt an image of unity, denying publicly any discord between Anglos and Hispanics: the official, "traditional" opening involves both the Rey Feo and King Antonio in front of the Alamo; they appear as time-honored descendants of the past, depicting, when placed together, the Mexican and Anglo heritage of the site.

The legacy of San Antonio embodied in descendants is what sells at Fiesta, which is purportedly a celebration of the region's past. People as descendants are part of the valued past, a concept developed to its fullest extent during Fiesta San Antonio. The different pasts revered at this festival—victory at San Jacinto versus pre-Anglo San Antonio—declare the popularity contest between the city's descendants; the favored heirs control the imagery of the festival.

Until the Hispanic rise in political power within the city, there was no contest; the Anglo Texans held the day (and the week), as anyone could tell who had listened to the past recounted at the Alamo. Fiesta marked the end of the six-week mourning period between the fall of the Alamo and victory at San Jacinto; it celebrated the movement of the Southwest into the preordained possession of the United States.

In this story line, the Alamo sacrifice becomes the reason that the Americans must ultimately be the masters of the plains. The land undergoes a social rebirth which is recounted in the Texas creation myth presented during Fiesta. In the eyes of the myth purveyors, all who participate in Fiesta San Antonio must acknowledge the Alamo's role in birthing Texas and that the Alamo sacrifice is the *raison d'être* of the April celebration. In this ideology, Fiesta must continue to mark the end of the chaos and backwardness characterizing Texas under Mexican dominance; to "the faithful," Fiesta San Antonio is the secular Easter six weeks after the Good Friday of the Alamo's fall.

# Chapter 3. Texas in Her Birth

Annual Alamo ceremonies occurring on March 6 and during Fiesta proclaim the creation of Texas. But in the annual cycle, the time between March 6 and April 21 is the gestational period for Texas. On March 6 Texas is engendered at the Battle of the Alamo, and she has her epiphany on April 21 when, after Sam Houston's victory at San Jacinto, the rest of the world recognizes Texas as an independent nation. During annual performances held in front of or inside the Alamo church, speakers recount the 1836 events from March 6 to April 21 as a unified narrative with the sacrificial fall of the Alamo and the victory at San Jacinto as the inseparable alpha and omega of the Texas creation mythology.

No group is more convinced of the interconnectedness of the battles than the Daughters of the Republic of Texas, the state-appointed custodians of the Alamo. In the introduction of speakers at the 1989 Pilgrimage to the Alamo (held on Monday of Fiesta week), one DRT member justified celebrating Fiesta in San Antonio by connecting the fall of the Alamo to the victory at San Jacinto:

We celebrate the San Jacinto victory here at the Alamo because the two . . . events are forever linked together. There was no real army in Texas in 1835 and '36, and given the developments in Texas at that time, it became necessary for William Barret Travis to devise a strategy at the Alamo, and that strategy was to keep Santa Anna occupied until General Houston could muster an army for the east. Travis was buying time for Houston, and that time was bought with the lives of the Alamo heroes. Had it not been for the delay here at the Alamo, the story would have been undoubtedly much different.

(1989 Pilgrimage to the Alamo)

According to this account of the Texas Revolution, the death of the Alamo defenders is a strategic and well-executed military move; as a successful sacrifice, the Alamo story ends with victory rather than defeat. Travis's decision to stay appears as a redeemed investment rather than a needless waste of human lives, the inception of a painful birth rather than of death. Within the mythology the Alamo harbors the metaphorical altar on which the Alamo defenders—led by the trinity of Travis, Bowie, and Crockett—offer their lives to allow this birth of Texas liberty. The old mission itself becomes part of the birthing process as it is reborn as a Texas shrine from its former fallen self, never again to be in the same family as its sister missions. In the words of one account of the battle, the Alamo was baptized in the fire of battle and the blood of heroes.

The sacred character of the Texas creation myth is portrayed in ceremonies performed in front of the Alamo by various groups. To understand the significance of details offered by these groups and the rituals performed, we must look at the entire myth. I offer the following compilation of favored details.

**The Texas Creation Myth.**   In December 1835, the city of San Antonio de Bexar was in the hands of the Mexican army under Gen. Martín Perfecto de Cos. Texan forces, camped outside of San Antonio, had been anxiously waiting for the command to attack for two months. But on December 3, to their disappointment, the Texan commander Gen. Edward Burleson ordered retreat. Ben Milam, a crusty old soldier serving under Burleson, despised the thought of retreating; on December 4 he stormed out of Burleson's tent, shouting, "Who will go with old Ben Milam to San Antonio?" Over two hundred cheering men rushed to join him. The next morning Milam led his men in house-to-house fighting with the Mexican army. One by one the enemy succumbed to the superior fighting skill of the Texans. On December 10, General Cos surrendered; the Texans had taken San Antonio.

But the victory had its price, for on December 7 the Texans' leader Ben Milam, hit by a bullet at the entrance to the governor's palace, became a sacrifice to the Texan cause. The Texans buried Milam in the courtyard of the house where his blood had hallowed the ground.

General Cos and his surviving troops were ordered to leave Texas and never to return. The Texans then began to prepare San Antonio's defense. The old mission compound of San Antonio de Valero, known as the Alamo, became the focus of the military strategists.

But Gen. Sam Houston, the commander of the entire Texas army, wanted the Texans in San Antonio to fall back and reinforce him and Col. James Fannin. So Houston sent James Bowie to San Antonio to destroy the Alamo. Bowie, however, could not bring himself to destroy the crumbling old mission. Perhaps he felt the power in the stones; perhaps he was simply considering his own landholdings, which lay near the city. Whatever the reason, he spared the Alamo. He declared that he would rather "die in these ditches" than leave San Antonio, and he worked with the Texans to transform the old Spanish mission into a Texan fortress.

Bowie was but the first Texan to feel drawn to the Alamo. William Barret Travis, upon his arrival on February 3, agreed with Bowie and the new commander of the Texans in San Antonio, Colonel Neill, that the Alamo would serve as a fortress and that San Antonio must be kept out of the Mexican army's hands.

Although Bowie and Travis agreed on where to make a military stand, they did not initially agree on who should be the garrison's commander after Colonel Neill was called away. Bowie, being almost twice Travis's age and well known for his fighting ability, felt he should hold the reins of authority. He had come to Texas long before Travis arrived there and had converted to Mexican citizenry and Catholicism as required by the Mexican government; he knew the people and the culture of San Antonio and Texas and had survived along with them in this frontier community. His prowess with the famed Bowie knife had made him a living legend.

Despite his triumphs of the past, however, Bowie was not at this time the powerful man he once had been. Sorrow over the deaths of his beautiful Mexican wife, Ursula Verimendi Bowie, and their children had led him to seek solace in the bottle. Now as he struggled with Travis to be commander, Bowie leaned heavily on alcohol. The young, headstrong Travis had no patience with Bowie's drunkenness and felt he was the more capable leader for the Texans. Travis knew in his heart that they were fighting for Texas' independence from Mexico, not to continue under the mother country's rule; the burden of taxes and the required Catholicism had made the yoke of Mexican citizenry unbearable. This fiery young South Carolinian withdrew from the drunken rampages being conducted by Bowie and his men throughout the city and moved his men into the Alamo compound. Bowie at last realized the damage he was doing to the Texan force and sent his apologies to young Travis. The two men settled on a joint command.

A man of great spirit soon joined Travis and Bowie in their desire to defend the Alamo: David Crockett. With his rifle Old Betsy in his arms and his Tennessee volunteers by his side, he rode into San Antonio a few days after Travis's arrival there. A veteran of the Creek

Indian wars, Crockett accepted Texas as his next mission in the settling of America's western frontier. Although Crockett was the same age as Bowie, he did not cling to his past. Rather he sought challenge on the frontier, and his arrival brought new life to the fatigued Texans.

But even as the Texans worked to ready the Alamo for her stand against the Mexican army, Gen. Antonio López de Santa Anna, the self-styled Napoleon of the West, marched toward Texas. If not the most brilliant of military strategists in history, Santa Anna was perhaps the most vain. The general's uniform contained enough silver on the epaulets and frogging for an entire set of dinner spoons; he rode on a saddle with gold-plated trim; and at his side hung a seven-thousand-dollar sword. He rode on toward Texas with the confidence that his massive army, drilled in European military maneuvers, would quickly bring the rebellious Texans to their knees.

Upon his arrival in San Antonio, Santa Anna had his men raise a blood-red banner above the San Fernando Cathedral bell tower signifying no quarter for the Alamo defenders. Travis boldly fired a cannon shot in response; he had made his decision to stay with the Alamo and defend her to the death. He then sent out his first appeal for aid from his fellow Americans. Through the ensuing days, he continued to appeal for help, and in his letter of February 24 Travis vowed, "I shall never surrender or retreat. . . . Victory or death."

But there was to be no help for the Alamo heroes, save thirty-two men from Gonzales who, determined to stand beside their countrymen, rushed through the Mexican lines and into the Alamo. Travis's appeals to the men at the Goliad garrison had failed; Goliad's woefully inept commander, Colonel Fannin, had decided, after a feeble attempt to march his men toward San Antonio, that he would not aid the Alamo defenders. And Sam Houston, despite his grave concern for the fate of the Alamo defenders, was in the eastern part of Texas trying to organize the major force of the Texas army; he needed every moment Travis and the Alamo defenders could buy him in their stalling of Santa Anna.

On March 3, James Bonham, Travis's messenger to Fannin, braved the run through enemy lines to report that Fannin would not come to their aid. Travis now faced the absolute desperation of their position. Two days later, Travis called his men before him and offered each man a choice: he could stay with Travis and defend the Alamo, selling his life dearly by destroying as many of the enemy as possible; or he could scale the Alamo's walls and try to slip through the Mexican lines. Travis then unsheathed his sword, drew its tip through the dirt in front of his men, and said, "Those prepared to give their lives in freedom's cause come over to me." Each Texan then made his choice, sealing his fate as he crossed over to Travis's side. Bowie, bedridden by a mysterious disease, called to the men to come and carry him across.

Only one man chose not to cross Travis's line: Louis (Moses) Rose. Rose, a Jewish Frenchman and veteran of the Napoleonic wars, declared that he had survived too many military encounters to lay down his life at the Alamo. He took his leave of the other men, scaled the Alamo wall, and disappeared into the darkness of the night.

That night, the twelfth one of the siege, Travis and his men slept peacefully for the first time since the siege had begun, for there was no gunfire from the Mexican lines. All was strangely quiet. But in the darkness, the Mexican soldiers crept into position, and lay waiting for the command to begin the final assault. As dawn streaked the sky with red, the battle cry "Viva Santa Anna" broke the peace, and out of the darkness wailed the trumpet notes of the dread *deguello*, whose title means "to slit the throat." Travis leapt from his bed and called his men to arms. He raced to meet the Mexican charge at the north wall. He spun around, a single bullet in his forehead, and slid dazed and dying against the embankment.

On the south side of the compound, David Crockett fired his rifle as long as he was able to reload her, and then swung Old Betsy as a war club, piling up the bodies at his feet before a saber cut him across the brow. He fell, Old Betsy in his arms.

In the Long Barracks Bowie lay ready in his sickbed to meet his final challenge. The door to his sickroom burst open, and Bowie fired his pistols, killing the first onslaught of Mexicans. Then with all his remaining strength he wielded his famed knife against those daring to come within arm's reach. At last the Mexicans crowding into the room pierced him with their bayonets and jubilantly lifted his body high above their heads.

Huddled in a front room of the Alamo church was Susanna Dickinson and her fourteen-month-old daughter, Angelina. One of the panicked defenders ran into the room pursued by Mexican soldiers. At Susanna's side he pleaded for his life, but was stabbed by several bayonets. The bloodthirsty Mexican soldiers lifted him up in the air on their bayonets and tossed his body like fodder, the man screaming in agony until he expired.

At last the Alamo compound fell silent; the 189 defenders lay dead. Santa Anna paraded on his horse through the battle site. One of his officers congratulated him on his great victory, and Santa Anna replied, "It was but a small affair."

But this was no small affair. Travis and his men had indeed sold their lives dearly. More than one thousand Mexican soldiers had fallen as casualties to the Texans' guns; so many that the Mexican officers were unable to carry out Santa Anna's order that all Mexican soldiers be given a Christian burial. Many bodies were simply thrown into the San Antonio River, where downstream they choked the waters and fouled the air with their stench. For days the sky was blackened with buzzards come to feed on the flesh.

By Santa Anna's command, the Alamo heroes received no Christian burial. Their bodies were stacked between layers of wood and burned. The flame from the funeral pyre rose high into the sky of early evening. The defenders had offered their lives as sacrifice on Freedom's altar; they had paid the ultimate price.

Though the Alamo heroes could not have known it, they had fought for what Travis had known would be the final goal of the Texas Revolution: an independent Republic of Texas. On March 2 the convention held at Washington-on-the-Brazos had voted to declare independence from Mexico. The duty of Travis and his men at the Alamo had become clear to the men at that historic convention.

Twelve days after the fall of the Alamo, the Mexican troops under General Urrea besieged the Texans at Goliad under Col. James Fannin. On March 20 Fannin decided that his situation was hopeless and surrendered his four hundred men, placing them "at the disposal of the Supreme Mexican government" and hoping for mercy. The men were forced into small, hot rooms and given tiny amounts of water and raw beef while Urrea awaited Santa Anna's sentence on the prisoners. Despite their desperate situation, many of the imprisoned Texans still hoped that they would be freed and allowed to go home. But on Palm Sunday, March 27, the four hundred prisoners were marched out on the open prairie and shot at point-blank range. The Mexican guards then stripped the bodies, stacked them, and burned them.

These were indeed dark days for Texas. Santa Anna's cruelty at the Alamo and Goliad spawned a reign of terror, and fear whipped across the young republic. Some soldiers abandoned the newly formed Texas army and raced home to gather loved ones and belongings. They then joined in the Runaway Scrape, a flood of people trying to outrun Santa Anna's army.

And it must have seemed at first glance that even Sam Houston was running away as he ordered his men to retreat. He knew he must still find more time to organize his military force and strategy if he were to end the tyranny of Santa Anna. His men cried out against what they felt was cowardice in the call to retreat. People along the way laughed at Sam Houston as he moved eastward. One old woman screamed scornfully, "Run, run, Santa Anna is behind you!" Even the republic's president, David Burnet, demeaned Houston, saying, "The Enemy are laughing you to scorn." And there were grumblings of mutiny among Houston's own men.

Only Houston could know the importance of his moves as he pulled his men farther into east Texas. When they arrived at the San Jacinto River, Houston carefully chose his campsite where he would allow Santa Anna to think that he had "trapped" the Texans. There he waited.

On April 20 Santa Anna sent his infantry to try the Texan lines, but the Texans repelled the infantry with the deadly fire of the Twin Sisters, two cannon sent by the citizens of Cincinnati to accompany Sam Houston into battle. Santa Anna then decided to pull his men back to camp, less than a mile from the Texan camp.

On April 21 both armies appeared ready for battle. But the Mexican army, even though it was much larger than Houston's, seemed to be waiting for even more troops to arrive. At half past three in the afternoon, Houston, after hearing that the Mexican soldiers had stacked their arms for *siesta*, decided the moment had arrived; he gave the command for Texans to advance on the Mexican lines.

Quietly they came, these angry men, resolved to avenge the unjust deaths of their countrymen. In the clear, bright afternoon sun, they advanced on the sleeping Mexicans without being seen even to within two hundred yards of the enemy.

Then from the enemy barricade a shot rang out, and the fighting began. "Fight for your lives!" cried the Texas officers. Sam Houston's voice roared commands, the Twin Sisters boomed, as the Texans charged the Mexican soldiers with wild whoops and screams: "Remember the Alamo! Remember Goliad!" The enraged Texans, though greatly outnumbered, fought with a fury deep within them.

In only eighteen minutes the battle was over. Knowing that all was lost for them, the Mexican soldiers broke and ran. Forlorn Mexican soldiers fell down before the vengeful Texans pleading "Me no Alamo. Me no Goliad." But there would be no excuses taken that day, no mercy given. The anger building in the six weeks since the Alamo had fallen raged inside the Texans; now the real killing began. With a score to settle, they took prisoners the way Santa Anna had done, dispatching them with Bowie knives, bullets, and gun butts.

Finally, at sundown, the killing subsided. The Texans, their anger spent, were finally able to follow Houston's orders to take prisoners instead of lives. Then the Texans began to count the losses: the Mexican army had killed 9 Texans; the Texans had killed 630 Mexicans.

But the victory was not complete, for Santa Anna had slipped away. Around noon the next day, Texans searching for stragglers found a man crawling through the grass near a destroyed bridge. He was dressed in common clothes and was wet and dirty. As the Texans brought this man into their camp, the other Mexican prisoners began calling out "El Presidente," pointing to this new prisoner. It was indeed Santa Anna, and the Texans took him immediately to Sam Houston. Houston, who had been wounded during the battle the day before, lay under an oak tree resting when the men brought Santa Anna before him. Santa Anna announced, "I am General Antonio López de Santa Anna, and a prisoner of war at your disposition." He then congratulated Houston, saying, "You have conquered the Napoleon of the West." As Santa Anna stood before Sam Houston, many of the Texans cried out for his execution. But Houston knew that he was not the authority within the new republic, and declared that the Texas Congress must decide the fate of Santa Anna. Furthermore, Sam Houston knew that Santa Anna was worth more alive than he would be dead, and so he wisely held on to the Texans' prize prisoner.

The justice dispensed by Sam Houston marked the reign of a new law in Texas. But the sovereignty of this new law would not have been possible without the sacrifice at the Alamo. Travis and his men paid the price of freedom; with their blood they bought time, vital time for Houston to organize. But more important, they gave the Texans the spirit to fight and the battle cry that drove the Texans forward and that made the Mexicans abandon all hope: "Remember the Alamo!" From the Alamo heroes' funeral pyre rose the spirit of sacrifice, freed from the flesh to embolden the hearts of the Texans at San Jacinto. And this spirit, present in every man who crossed Travis's line, engendered within that old mission, the newly born fortress—Texas liberty. Their bravery inspired Gen. Thomas Jefferson Green to declare, "Thermopylae had her messenger of defeat; the Alamo had none."

Table 3.1 shows the frequency with which certain details of the myth appear in various types of history texts. I have divided the texts into five categories. The section labeled "Juvenile" contains those written for (and, in one case, by) schoolchildren. The "Historians" section contains texts written for a general audience but with an academic intent (education as opposed to entertainment). But the tone of these texts is often difficult to distinguish from that of texts appearing in popular journals, particularly the tone in Lon Tinkle's work; thus the distinction between this category and that of "Popular" is somewhat arbitrary, the main distinction being that the "Popular" are those appearing in popular magazines or guidebooks. The "Local" section contains those aimed at Texans and appearing in Texas newspapers and other Texas publications. Many local versions use expected background knowledge of the battle to make their effects felt, especially Mike Kelley's "Edited for Length: Alamo Cut from Epic to Mini-Miniseries." The dates on most of these histories are significant (i.e., they are published during the liminal period or on the anniversary of one battle or the other). The section "Debunkers" contains two attempts to debunk the Texas creation myth, especially the success imagery of the Alamo battle. The final section, "Films," contains two popular film versions of the Alamo story, John Wayne's *The Alamo*, produced in 1960, and *Alamo . . . The Price of Freedom*, produced in 1988.

The texts within each section are merely a sampling of such texts. (This is *by no means* an exhaustive survey of all the historical texts ever written about the Battle of the Alamo and its place within the Texas Revolution.) I have tried to draw the texts examined from a wide time frame (1874–1990). Within each section the texts appear in chronological order, with the earliest text first.

The Texas creation myth depicts the violent birth of a new nation, Texas; the Alamo is the cradle of this nation and source of her liberty. On the metaphorical altar within the Alamo walls the Alamo heroes offer their lives. Through their violent deaths, the Alamo is born to a new life, "with almost every stone baptized in human blood, shed in the defence of liberty" (Gould 1883:3). The mythic baptismal font flows with the blood of the Alamo heroes, the life-giving fluid from which Texas liberty is born. Their blood waters the ground where Travis has sown the seed of the new nation, and she arises, "springing forth from the flow of the martyrs' blood" (*Good Roads* 1914:3).

Within the mythology, the Alamo defenders' blood is the baptizing current for the Alamo and nourishment for the seed of Texas liberty. But a close look at the exchange metaphors offered in several versions of the Alamo story reveals that the heroes' blood also serves as currency with which Travis and the rest of the defenders purchase (1) time and (2) land. The heroes "pay" for Texas' independence from Mexico with their lives. (The DRT continues this transaction by "paying tribute" and thereby retaining the right to administer the site.) In the speech by the DRT member quoted earlier in

**Table 3.1.** *Occurrence of Details in Various History Texts*

KEY
g — ground
nr — nothing referenced
ds — dust
dr — dirt
f — floor
e — earth
s — sand

| | PENNYBACKER 1907 | DAFFAN 1908 | SMITH 1924 | LOWMAN 1942 | MOFFITT 1953 | JAKES 1986 | PEARSON 1987 | ALAMO TOUR 1990 |
|---|---|---|---|---|---|---|---|---|
| INITIAL SACRIFICE OF BEN MILAM | * | * | * | * | * | | * | |
| SANTA ANNA AS NAPOLEON/CORRUPT | * | * | * | | | | * | |
| BLOOD-RED BANNER | | * | | * | * | * | * | * |
| CANNON-SHOT RESPONSE | | * | | * | | | * | * |
| TRAVIS'S APPEALS FOR HELP | * | | * | * | * | * | | |
| HELP DENIED | * | | | | | | * | |
| TRAVIS'S LINE | | *g | | | | | *g | *g |
| *DEGUELLO* PLAYED | * | | | | * | * | * | |
| DARKNESS AT FALL OF ALAMO | * | | | | | * | * | * |
| TRAVIS'S DEATH | * | * | | * | * | | * | * |
| CROCKETT'S DEATH | | | | * | | | * | * |
| BOWIE'S DEATH | | | | * | | * | * | * |
| SANTA ANNA'S COMMENT | | | | | | | * | |
| NUMBER SLAIN | | | | * | | * | * | |
| FUNERAL PYRE | * | * | | | * | | * | * |
| CRUELTY AT GOLIAD | * | * | | | | | * | |
| RUNAWAY SCRAPE | * | * | | | | * | * | |
| HOUSTON'S RETREAT | * | | | | | | * | |
| SLEEPING MEXICAN ARMY | * | * | | | | * | * | |
| SAVAGERY OF TEXANS | * | * | * | | | * | * | |
| EXCUSES OFFERED | * | * | * | | | * | * | |
| CAPTURE OF SANTA ANNA | * | | * | | | * | * | |
| HOUSTON'S JUSTICE | * | * | * | | | | | |
| POSITIVE EFFECTS | * | * | * | * | * | | * | * |
| BATTLE CRY | * | * | * | * | * | * | * | * |
| THERMOPYLAE SAYING | *her | | | | | | | |

JUVENILE

| LITHERINGTON 1874 | TINKLE 1953 | LORD 1961 | PROCTOR 1986 | GOULD 1883 | HUMBLE OIL 1936 | MULLER 1940 | BANKS 1952 | RAY 1955 | WARREN 1958 | DOBIE 1959 | PARADE 1987 | MCALISTER 1988 | GOOD ROADS 1914 | S.A. LIGHT 1936 | PUGH 1986 | KELLEY 1990 | MCWILLIAMS 1978 | LONG 1990 | WAYNE 1960 | MERRILL 1988 |
|---|---|---|---|---|---|---|---|---|---|---|---|---|---|---|---|---|---|---|---|---|
|  | * |  | * | * | * |  |  | * | * |  |  | * | * |  |  |  |  | * |  |  |
|  | * | * | * |  |  | * |  | * | * |  | * | * | * |  |  |  |  | * |  |  |
|  | * | * | * | * |  |  |  | * | * |  | * | * |  |  | * |  |  | * | * | * |
| * | * | * | * | * |  | * |  | * | * |  |  | * | * |  | * |  |  | * | * | * |
| * | * | * | * | * | * | * | * | * | * |  |  | * | * |  | * | * |  | * | * | * |
|  | * | * | * | * |  | * |  | * | * |  | * | * | * | * | * |  |  | * | * | * |
|  | *nr | *nr | *g | *nr | *g | *ds | *f | *e | *ds |  | *ds | *dr | *nr | *nr | *dr | *nr | *s | *dr |  | * |
| * | * |  | * | * | * |  | * |  | * |  |  | * | * | * |  | * |  | * | * | * |
|  |  | * | * |  |  |  |  | * | * |  | * | * |  | * |  |  |  |  |  | * |
| * | * | * | * | * | * | * |  | * |  |  |  | * | * |  | * |  | * | * | * | * |
| * | * | * | * | * | * | * |  | * |  |  |  | * | * |  | * |  | * | * | * | * |
| * | * | * |  | * | * | * |  | * |  |  |  | * | * |  |  |  | * | * | * | * |
|  |  | * | * |  |  |  |  |  | * |  |  | * | * |  | * |  |  | * |  |  |
| * | * | * | * | * | * |  |  |  | * |  |  | * | * | * | * |  |  | * |  | * |
|  | * | * |  |  |  |  |  |  | * |  |  |  |  |  | * |  |  | * |  | * |
|  | * |  |  |  |  | * |  |  | * |  |  |  |  |  |  |  |  | * |  |  |
|  | * |  |  |  |  |  |  |  | * |  |  |  |  |  |  |  |  | * |  |  |
|  | * |  |  |  | * | * |  |  | * |  |  |  |  |  |  |  |  | * |  |  |
|  | * |  | * |  |  |  |  |  | * |  |  |  |  |  |  |  |  | * |  |  |
|  | * |  | * |  |  |  |  |  | * |  |  |  |  |  |  |  |  | * |  |  |
|  | * |  |  |  |  | * |  |  |  |  |  |  |  |  |  |  |  | * |  |  |
| * | * | * | * | * | * | * |  |  |  |  | * | * |  |  | * | * | * | * |  | * |
|  | * | * |  | * | * | * | * | * | * |  | * | * |  |  | * |  |  | * |  |  |
| *three | *her |  | * |  |  |  |  | *her |  |  |  |  | *her |  |  |  |  |  |  |  |
| HISTORIANS |  |  |  | POPULAR |  |  |  |  |  |  |  |  | LOCAL |  |  |  | DEBUNKERS |  | FILMS |  |

this chapter, she states: "Travis was buying time for Houston, and that time was bought with the lives of the Alamo heroes." According to the mythology, time is a quantitative commodity, and Travis and his men purchase thirteen days' worth.

The land obtained in the exchange is also quantifiable in the number of acres that make up Texas. The image of defined land purchased with blood appears in the poem by Marvin Davis Winsett recited at the 1990 DRT March 6 memorial service; in this poem Winsett declares Travis, Crockett, Bowie, and Bonham to be men who paid for "this plot of earth with their own blood."[1] The "plot of earth" gives the impression of defined farmland with individual ownership.

Within the mythology, the heroes' blood simultaneously purchases the land and waters the fertile earth where they have sown the seed of Texas liberty. Travis, as director of this purchase, appears as an astute businessman, wisely investing his life and those of his men to "buy" time and finally land. As the title of the new IMAX film states, the sacrifice at the Alamo is "the price of freedom." But if we look carefully at the entire Texas creation myth, we see that Texas is already rightfully in the hands of the Texans at the time of the Alamo battle. Ben Milam has already paid the price with his blood, or at least he has given a down payment on the land with his life. The popular inclusion of Ben Milam's death is vital to making Travis and his men "defenders" of the Alamo. Rather than the Texans appearing as invaders who simply usurp power, they rightfully possess Texas, according to the myth, at the time of the Alamo battle because of Ben Milam's sacrifice. Within this script, Santa Anna and the Mexican army are the invaders coming in to destroy order and steal what rightfully belongs to the Texans.

The men inside the Alamo are also "defenders" in the concept of "Manifest Destiny" supported in the nineteenth century: Texas was destined to be part of the United States. Perhaps as Manifest Destiny has retreated as a means of justifying the taking of Texas and the rest of what is now the American Southwest, the sacrifice of Ben Milam has become a more popular means of making Travis and the others defenders.[2]

The death of the Alamo defenders (in terms of both Manifest Destiny and initial sacrifice) at the hands of the Mexican army marks an inversion of the proper order, one that is righted only after the Battle of San Jacinto. The scenario is similar to the fall of a heavenly ruler as described by Marshall Sahlins: the world "dissolves," and chaos reigns until the rightful successor "returns to reinstate the tabus and redivide lands—i.e., to recreate the differences that make up the natural and cultural order" (Sahlins 1985:43). With the entrance of Santa Anna, order, the cultural influence brought by the Texans, is lost, and chaotic fear pervades the land.

In the mythology, the chaos that Santa Anna brings is corruption—Old World corruption—as revealed in his association with Napoleon. He is European culture gone bad, dripping and rotting with excess, which becomes the perversion of culture. Santa Anna is death incarnate, as revealed in his order that the "blood-red banner" of no quarter be flown. But, according to the mythology, death has no power over Travis, as is apparent in his defiant cannon-shot response; he is committed to standing against death.

Once Travis has committed himself to this task, he becomes similar to Christ in the Garden of Gethsemane: although Travis calls out for help, there is no one to "take this cup" from him. He realizes that his sacrifice must be carried out; he has already crossed the line separating the living and the dead. He then asks his men to cross that line as well.[3]

The defenders as a group become, mythologically, the divine sacrifice for the Texas cause, and in crossing Travis's line they have agreed to be sacrificed on "the altar of Liberty" (Gould 1883:22; cf. also Moffitt 1953:19). As in ancient fertility rites, Travis has plowed a furrow with his sword in the dirt and has planted the seed of Texas liberty with his words. The sacrificial blood will then water this seed, it will emerge from the martyrs' blood, and it will bear fruit at the Battle of San Jacinto.

It is important to note that in the texts charted above words denoting fertile land—dirt, earth, ground—are used in reference to the substance in which Travis draws his sword more than twice as frequently as words suggesting a soil lacking fertility—dust and sand. The mythology declares that in the hands of Travis and the Texans this land will produce rather than lie as a crumbling wasteland.

But the planting of the seed of Texas liberty and the new nation offers only potential; nourishment by blood is essential if it is to emerge. In the mythology, Travis and his men understand this need and prepare for the sacrificial death that brings new life. To this end, the Texans *allow* the Mexican army to carry out this sacrifice; it is the Texans' choice to die rather than the Mexicans' choice to defeat them.

There is an unnatural quiet as this intended inversion of order begins. Santa Anna and the Mexican army prepare for the final role of high priest of the sacrifice. Darkness, broken only by streaks of red, foretelling the blood to flow, surrounds the fall of the heavenly rulers. The Mexican army rides on the wave of fear, swelling with the notes of the *deguello* and the cries in Spanish praising this Mexican prince of darkness. According to the mythology, cruelty is the norm as the Mexican soldiers ghoulishly carry out their role. Death and chaos reign. After the fall of the Alamo, the normally clear water and air become fouled by death, and carrion seekers darken the skies.

Inversion in the mythology continues during the period between March 6 and April 21: Fannin and the Texans with him surrender rather than fight; soldiers who have willingly surrendered receive cruel treatment and execution rather than mercy; would-be brave Texans abandon home and army, joining in the Runaway Scrape; Houston, who deserves the respect and obedience of his men, is mocked for his seeming cowardice; and the Mexican soldiers enjoy the abandoned goods of the Anglo settlers, elements of culture the Texans rightfully own.

The finale of inversion in the mythology comes in the savagery of the Texans as they overrun the Mexicans during their *siesta*. In this reversal, the Texans are the purveyors of death, cruelty, and terror. They run without order, creating chaos throughout the battlefield; they utter "wild" screams and refuse the pleading prisoners mercy; and they ignore the orders of their commanders. Inversion stops only after anger is spent. Then they begin to follow the orders of their commanders and act in a humane fashion toward the Mexican prisoners.

This return to order in the mythology brings a return of rightful status with the Texans as captors and guards and the Mexicans as prisoners. Santa Anna's cultural veneer is stripped away, and he shrinks in the shadow of the Texans' charge. He is stripped of his finery, save his slippers and underwear; he becomes a foolish figure rather than an embodiment of terror, a laughable varmint rather than a fearsome monster. He flees from the battle, and later crawls like a serpent through grass in an attempt to escape.[4]

When Santa Anna is brought to face the victor (Sam Houston), he expects to be murdered by the men who hold him or upon the order of Houston. But, as proper order has returned, Houston recognizes that justice lies not in an individual's hands but in the legislative body; he sends his prisoner to face the higher power of this civilized land, the Texas Congress. A new culture reigns.

According to the mythology, this transition to a new order is due in part to a fatal flaw within the old culture: *siesta* in the middle of the day. The Mexican soldiers have stacked their arms when they should be ready to use them. This cultural deficiency stands in con-trast to the high productivity of the Texans expressed in the number of Mexicans they kill. Several versions of the Texas creation myth state with pride the number of Mexicans killed versus the number of Texans killed. This juxtaposing of the war dead creates a scoring technique which allows the Texans to "win" both at the Alamo and at San Jacinto. This conceit is exemplified in the essay by a high school student (Lowman 1942); opting for a conservative estimate of the Mexican casualties at the Alamo, Shepard Lowman states, "The more conservative figure of from three hundred to four hun-dred seems to need no enlarging to make it a tremendous score for the defenders" (Lowman 1942:11).

The favorite score within the mythology is that of the San Jacinto encounter; what a rout! The Texans are obviously superior on the field. The continuing awareness of the scoring is apparent in Leo Garza's political cartoon of April 1991 (Fig. 3.1). The scoring ap-proach is particularly significant when we consider that the Texas public school system indoctrinates its students in Texas history dur-ing seventh grade, about the same age level that football compe-tition becomes heated in the schools; scoring is all-important. In Garza's cartoon the triumphant, buckskin-clad Texan figure sug-

Fig. 3.1. Cartoon 1 by Leo Garza.
*Reprinted by permission of Leo Garza.*

gests Crockett who piles up the bodies, or runs up the points, by his prowess on the field.[5]

But the leaders of such warriors, Travis and Houston, do not measure their value in the number of men they kill. Houston is the implementor of the new law, one in which justice is determined by the state rather than by an individual. Although Houston is ridiculed during the liminal period, he knows that he is the rightful commander within Texas and that the new order as embodied within him will ultimately rule Texas. Mythologically, it is for this new order of justice and government that Travis has laid down his life; he is the fate-ordained sacrifice for the new law of the land.

Within the mythology, all Texans are united in their quest for this justice; to this end there are no dissenters within the ranks, even among the Alamo defenders. For that reason, some historians interpret the saying "Thermopylae had her messenger of defeat; the Alamo had none" to mean that no one at the Alamo turned traitor to lend aid to Santa Anna in defeating the Texans.[6] But a more common interpretation of this saying is that the Alamo defenders "did Thermopylae one better"; the Texans lost *all* their men in the battle.[7] But at least one DRT representative has protested the saying on the grounds that the Alamo *did* have a messenger of defeat: Susanna Dickinson. However, her status as messenger is not recognized because women are not significant within the battle imagery of this story line.

In the mythology, the Texans possess the cultural and technological wisdom necessary to clear Texas of barriers to productivity; reproductivity must wait. Sacrifice is the order of the hour. With sacrifice as goal, the Alamo again does Thermopylae one better, because according to this mythology, it is not a defeat but a successful sacrifice; there can be no messenger of defeat if there is no defeat.

In this sacrifice, the young Travis and the defenders give their lives so that Texas may live. Alamo historian Paul Hutton notes similarities to the concept of ultimate sacrifice for the good of the world. In Susan Schoelwer's book *Alamo Images*, Hutton states that the Alamo story "embraces themes of courage, sacrifice, betrayal, and redemption. Its trinity of heroes—Travis, Bowie and Crockett—have since been deified beyond recognition as mere mortals" (Hutton [in Schoelwer] 1985 : 4–5).

There are correspondences between the three main heroes at the Alamo and the figures within the Christian Trinity. The interrelationships of the three reflect the perceived progression of Texas from her ancient past to her current status. Examining the three heroes and their related identities within the trinity allows us to understand the mythological metamorphosis whereby Texas sheds her past to become what she is.

In the mythology surrounding the Alamo the ancient past combines with the puritan of the western frontier and with the cavalier of the South to create Texas. Texas' past civilization, the western frontier, and the American South have corresponding figures who form a revered trinity. The Alamo trinity's structure parallels that of the Christian Trinity, which consists of the Father (the ancient ancestor), who engenders the second figure (the Son), who brings the new order to the world and who is engendered through the third figure (the Spirit) within a platonic woman. In the Alamo trinity James Bowie corresponds to the ancient father, Travis the son (the young sacrifice who brings the civilizing law), and David Crockett the ageless spirit.

The ancient father image explains the old order within Texas and why it must surrender its command to the new. James Bowie is the embodiment of ancient warfare and the past. At the time of the Texas Revolution, Bowie was already a legendary warrior. His hand-to-hand combat with a knife represents the savagery needed to survive in the primeval darkness of the Louisiana swamps, an ability he carries with him to the Texas frontier. Knife fighting requires a close contact with one's adversary, allowing a more intimate relationship between the combatants than does the frontier rifle.

Bowie's weapon is as primordial as he, as is revealed in folklorist J. Frank Dobie's description of the Bowie knife:

Through long centuries of warring, certain weapons of the Old World, like King Arthur's "Excalibur" and Siegmund's great sword "Gram," became the subjects of legends and of songs that have made them immortal. The solitary counterpart in the New World, before six-shooter and law-abiding habits supplanted its use, was the Bowie knife.

(Dobie 1953:33)

Dobie likens the legends of the knife's origin to those telling "how the dwarf smiths forged for the old Norse gods" (Dobie 1953:33).

Even in the early histories of the Alamo, Bowie is the ancient past. He is the most untamed man in the Alamo: "[H]e was a typical product of the wild Southwest in its wildest days . . . a man who had slain a hundred enemies, . . . who feared absolutely nothing, and who was as reckless in his anger as he could be in his generosity"

(Titherington 1874:345). Bowie's image is that of the ancient hero. He must use primitive means to survive desperate times. Of the men in the Alamo trinity, Bowie is the most closely related to the distant past and its *wilderness*.

Bowie's connection to the ancestral past pervades all his mythologized stages of life. When he moves to Texas, he associates with the established order within the region; he becomes part of Old San Antonio living in colorful antiquity. According to record, he became a Mexican citizen, converted to Catholicism, and married a Canary Island descendant; that is, he married into one of the established families in San Antonio. As the Texas Revolution nears, Bowie's "Mexican ways," according to historian Lon Tinkle, become a point of departure between him and other Texas colonists who favor independence from Mexico (Tinkle 1958:77). Bowie is thus married to a culture and a time more than to an individual. This "marriage" becomes more apparent when Ursula Verimendi Bowie and the Bowie children die.[8] After a period away in mourning, Bowie returns to San Antonio because, according to Tinkle, "the spell of Texas was upon him. . . . The land . . . could become a wife to a man—yes, a wife, and a child, too" (Tinkle 1958:81, 82).

This "marriage" to the land during Mexican rule in Texas is significant, for Mexico is often referred to as the "mother country" prior to Texas' independence; Bowie, as father figure, is still married to the mother country. Both become part of the ancestral past once the move for independence begins. Part of Bowie's father image, however, departs from the image of God the Father: Bowie, as a mortal, succumbs to the aging process, appearing frail in comparison to the youthful Travis. Bowie takes on the characteristics of the ailing father who, though past his prime, struggles to maintain his position of authority. Certainly at the time of the Alamo battle, Bowie appears as one no longer able to provide leadership. He at first wrestles with Travis for authority, then agrees to a joint command. He is finally confined to his bed and forced by illness to "surrender" full command to Travis.

Bowie will ultimately accept Travis's offer of salvation by crossing his line in the dirt. *It is important to note that Bowie must be carried across by the other men.* He is the past, married to the mother country, and is unable to cross the line on his own.

But at least Bowie makes it across the line to the new order. Moses Rose does not. Rose is the old order, being both Jewish and European. In the mythology, he is similar to Judas in the Gospels who, though initially part of Christ's inner circle, abandons Christ and his disciples in their darkest hour.[9]

Bowie's image as the dying commander is juxtaposed to the youthful Travis, the second figure in our trinity. Whereas Bowie's time of love, family, and fortune has passed, Travis's life lies ahead of him. Bowie has nothing left to lose; Travis has everything and is thus the most fitting member of the trinity to serve as sacrificial victim. He is the "paladin extraordinary" who, according to George McAlister, "favored clothes for his legal practice and social occasions instead of the usual rough boots and other frontier garb worn by most of the local men" (McAlister 1988a: 59, 91). Travis is the "red-haired stranger" (McAlister 1988a: 59); that is, he is different from the others in Texas at the time, and he comes in from the outside to bring a new order to Texas.[10]

As mentioned previously, Travis takes on a Christ-like aura in his decision to die at the Alamo and in his ability to extract the same commitment from the men of the garrison; all gain immortality in following Travis. This "transformative power of war," apparent in the Texas creation mythology, is part of a widely held view of battle sites as places of such transformation. Edward Linenthal, a professor of religious studies, explores this power:

> Conspicuous by their presence on the martial landscape are battlefields, prime examples of a sacred patriotic space where memories of the transformative power of war and the sacrificial heroism of the warrior are preserved.
>
> (Linenthal 1991: 3)

The mythologized transformation of the Alamo trinity figures, especially Travis's transformation, is a particularly poignant example of such power. He, more than any of the other men within the Alamo, becomes the sacrifice necessary to bring life to an independent Texas. Birth is, according to the nineteenth-century mind-set in which these legends arose, an extremely dangerous yet productive process. In some births, the mother dies (sacrifices herself) to produce a child. Similarly, Travis dies in the process of birthing Texas.

If Travis is the right man at the right place for a sacrificial beginning of the Southwest, it is the westward movement embodied in the third trinity figure which brings him there. David Crockett is the spirit of the West who fills the men of the garrison with the conviction that they are right and that they should go ahead. Formed of the same Puritan ideology that immortalized Daniel Boone, Crockett is the frontiersman who must work hard at surviving as well as at clearing the way for future colonists.

Even though Crockett displays ferocity in battle, he is not the wil-

derness spirit James Bowie is. A model frontier hero, Crockett serves
as a mediator between the old order and the new and between savagery and civilization.[11] He shares the frontiersman image with
Bowie; but he respects the ordered world of military ranks, and offers to submit, as a private, to the new order as embodied in Colonel
Travis.

As the model frontier hero, Crockett must quantitatively assess
his worth in numbers of bears, Indians, and Mexicans he can kill.
This productivity appears in Lon Tinkle's description of Crockett's
successes:

> Davy was the champion sharpshooter; in one season back in
> Tennessee he killed 109 bears. Some of these, of course, may
> have been in hand-to-hand combat, but Davy Crockett had al-
> ready staked his claim to number-one marksmanship. He had
> picked off the first Mexican on the first day. He didn't imagine
> the Texans would find enough guns to take care of all the
> notches he was going to cut. *The scoring was just starting* [em-
> phasis added]. He intended to surpass himself.
>
> (Tinkle 1958:118)

Crockett is the high scorer in this war tally. Tinkle's inclusion of
bears and Mexicans within the same paragraph reveals a mythological equation of the two as proper targets of Crockett's frontier rifle
and as numbers to be counted in assessing Crockett's worth.

Crockett, as high scorer in the battle, adds to the sacrifice image
of Travis: not only are the Alamo heroes the sacrificial victims; they
are also the sacrificers, surrounded by the bodies of enemy soldiers
sacrificed at their deaths. In this sacrifice/sacrificer duality, Travis
exemplifies the successful, life-giving sacrifice, and Crockett exemplifies the sacrificer who exacts a heavy toll from those who would
kill these Texas heroes.

Thus sacrifice in the Texas creation mythology both confirms the
transformation of Travis and the other defenders to the realm of the
sacred from the profane and serves as recompense for the wrong
done in inverting the proper order of the universe. Although Texans
play both roles of sacrificer and sacrifice in the Alamo battle, Texans
fill only the sacrificer role at the Battle of San Jacinto. Folklorist
Sylvia Grider refers to the "score" at San Jacinto as the legends'
means of portraying the Texans as "exacting almost divine retribu-
tion upon the Mexicans for what they did to the Texans at the
Alamo and Goliad" (Grider 1989:no pagination). In the depictions

of this battle, the concept of righting wrongs serves to justify the killing of so many unarmed Mexican soldiers.

With the roles of spirit, sacrificial son, and father filled by Crockett, Travis, and Bowie, respectively, the issue remains of platonic female vessel with whom the spirit conjoins to allow the birth of the new order. McAlister's description of Crockett's arrival on the scene best reveals the woman in this role: "In his foxskin [sic] cap . . . with old Betsy cradled in his arms, he appeared bigger than life itself. He was just the tonic needed at the right time" (McAlister 1988a:140). In actuality, Crockett had left his famous rifle in Tennessee. *Old Betsy was not at the Alamo at the time of the 1836 battle.* But she's there now, entombed in a glass case dedicated to David Crockett. And she's there in the narratives, the ever faithful wilderness companion to Crockett. As part of the violent birth, she stands in opposition to reproductive women, as she is an instrument of death meant to rid the West of barriers so that productivity can flourish. She is paralleled in the Battle of San Jacinto by the two cannon sent from Cincinnati, the Twin Sisters, who accompany Sam Houston into battle.[12]

These Texas "women" of cold metal are asensual beings who allow the Texas men to become masters of the field. Within the Texas creation myth, real men hold steel women. By giving guns women's names, men portray their perceived ability to control the power of life (and death) that is the "nature" of biological women.

In the Texas creation mythology, it is specifically Anglo men who control this power of women. It is interesting to note that the Texans' cannon which the Mexican soldiers turn upon the Texans in their storming of the Alamo have no names. The *named* steel women—Old Betsy and the Twin Sisters—remain in the hands of the Texans at all times. These "women" are technological rather than biological, and the Anglos, according to the mythology, possess the better women.

In possessing these women, the Anglo men control life and death via technological superiority. This possession of steel women ideologically mirrors men's possession of biological women, a presumption which is very much alive at the end of the twentieth century (otherwise, it would not survive in the mythology).[13] In declaring male possession of women, the reproductivity of women—a power which men do not possess in and of themselves—comes under male control, thus suggesting that men have both productivity and reproductivity as their dominion.

The Anglo men, that is. Social boundaries within the Texas creation mythology declare that both types of women (technological and biological) owe their fealty to Anglo men. When Hispanic men attempt to control biological women by engaging them (or trying to engage them) in sexual relationships, women bring about the downfall of these men. In its portrayal of the Hispanic male's inability to control the power of women, the Texas creation mythology dictates who is superior—technologically, biologically, and socially.

# Chapter 4. Ethnic Eves and Anglo Marys

Narratives of the Texas Revolution do not frequently mention women, primarily because most accounts of this time period focus on military events. Women are not usually associated with battle, even when they are present in the battle arena. But when women do appear in the narratives, their depictions generally follow patterns congruent with the social categories of the Texas creation mythology. According to this mythology, women, especially Anglo women, faithfully support Anglo men, but they serve as the nemesis of any Hispanic male who may seek to possess them.

The most famous legend about women in the Texas Revolution involves Santa Anna's mythological tryst with a beautiful mulatto slave named Emily Morgan, who is also known as the Yellow Rose of Texas. The following version of this legend is a compilation of favored details from oral and written versions of the Emily Morgan story. Quotations are from either the 1988 version by George McAlister, appearing in his book *A Time to Love . . . A Time to Die: A Tale of the Men Who Forged the Republic of Texas—Their Lives and Loves*, or the 1972 version by R. Henderson Shuffler entitled "San Jacinto, as She Was: Or, What Really Happened on the Plain of St. Hyacinth on a Hot April Afternoon in 1836."

Emily Morgan was a beautiful nineteen-year-old mulatto slave at the time of the Texas Revolution, and she belonged to Col. James Morgan, owner of a large plantation in an area known as Morgan's Point near New Washington. She was a "winsome, light-skinned product of the bedroom integration that was so popular in the South of that period" (Shuffler 1972:123). Although born a slave, Emily, according to fate's design, would play a major role in the battle between Santa Anna and Sam Houston.

Santa Anna, upon reaching Morgan's plantation on his march east, immediately noticed Emily, who had been left with the other slaves to take care of the plantation when Colonel Morgan fled before the advancing Mexican army. Santa Anna, a notorious womanizer, made no pretense about his desire for this young woman. And Emily may well have returned Santa Anna's interest, for he was considered a handsome man, and certainly attractive to such a woman as Emily, "a gal on the make" who "had been bedded many times" (McAlister 1988b:207). She was a good match for Santa Anna as she had "an unsatiable love for, and a certain expertise at, the art of sex" (McAlister 1988b:208).

Santa Anna took Emily and a mulatto slave boy named Turner with him on his march toward San Jacinto. He ordered Turner to go spy on the Texans, but Emily pulled Turner aside and asked him instead to report to Sam Houston concerning the location and strength of Santa Anna's army. As they were good friends, Turner did as Emily requested.

Upon reaching the San Jacinto area, Santa Anna chose a campsite that was poorly situated militarily but offered a romantic view of the San Jacinto Bay. Shortly after they had set up camp, Emily and Santa Anna disappeared into his tent.

In the meantime, Turner reported all to Houston regarding Santa Anna's position, strength, and his recent infatuation with Emily. A report from Houston's scout Deaf Smith further convinced Houston that Santa Anna was indeed preoccupied with a woman; Smith also reported that the Mexican soldiers had stacked their arms and were resting. With this information in mind, Houston decided the time had come for the Texans to take their revenge.

Around half past three that afternoon, the Texas army crept up on the unprepared Mexicans. They were within two hundred yards of the Mexican soldiers before they began firing. Santa Anna rushed from his tent in only a linen shirt and his underwear. He jumped on a stallion named Old Whip, which, instead of carrying Santa Anna to safety, bolted for his home barn on a ranch near the battlefield. Santa Anna then hid in the barn, where he found some old clothes to wear.

Santa Anna was captured the next day and became a prisoner of the Texas army. But no one really knows what happened to Emily Morgan. She may have been killed in the confusion, or she may have escaped. But her fame grew throughout Texas. If Santa Anna's roving eye had not fallen on her, he might not have lost at San Jacinto. "It was she who caused the 'Napoleon of the West' to rush onto the battlefield . . . in his silken drawers too late to rally his troops and too befuddled and bedwhipped to really understand what was going on" (McAlister 1988b:213). Santa Anna paid a high price for his time with Emily. "It can be accurately said that Emily swapped her questionable virtue for approximately a million square miles of the American West, which comes close to an all-time high in the market for the most ancient of commercial products" (Shuffler 1972:122).

Shuffler and McAlister each suggest in their conclusions that a monument should be made and dedicated to Emily Morgan. McAlister's book includes a drawing of his proposed monument in which Santa Anna stands in his military jacket and long underwear, which is unbuttoned at his genitals; with his left hand he is picking petals off a rose centered over Emily Morgan's genitals. She has only a sheet draped around her. She looks downward and away, and her hands are clasped behind her back in a posture of surrender. In his right hand Santa Anna holds a likeness of Texas (in its current, familiar shape) which is fragmenting and falling out of his grip. Below the figures are the following inscriptions:

In Honor and Memory  
of SANTA ANNA  
Holder of the World's Record  
in the Price Paid  
for Sexual Pleasure

In Honor and Memory  
of EMILY MORGAN  
"The Yellow Rose"  
Who Gave Her All for Texas  
Petal, by Petal, by Petal

McAlister then declares his proposed shrine "a fitting climax to this tale of love and history" (McAlister 1988b:214–215).

McAlister's version closely follows Henderson Shuffler's version (at times, almost word for word). Shuffler's proposed monument for Emily Morgan has an almost identical inscription regarding her role in the Texas Revolution:

In Honor of Emily  
Who Gave Her All for Texas  
Piece by Piece

In this inscription, "piece," of course, takes on its slang meaning of an act of copulation. Perhaps Shuffler's use of "piece" gave McAlister the idea of having Texas slipping in "pieces" out of Santa Anna's grip.

Both male authors depict Emily Morgan as sexuality personified. In McAlister's words, she is "a gal on the make" who has "an unsatiable love" for sex. Emily entices and then sexually consumes Santa Anna, leaving him unable to understand what is happening around him. Santa Anna, in Emily's arms, is diminished. By giving in to

Emily Morgan's sexual advances, this most prominent Mexican male falls in stature and loses Texas.

In the Emily Morgan legend we have one of the two avenues femininity can take in western mythologies. In this first option, woman is a temptress, luring man away from his proper duties. This image of woman and its antithesis derive, as in the case of the Alamo male trinity, from Christian ideology. For female characters, the roles available are part of the Judeo-Christian dichotomy of evil Eve and the virtuous Virgin Mary. Women in the Texas creation mythology are either purely sexual beings who tempt men and bring the downfall of those who become involved with them or they are faithful, asexual beings who believe in the eventual victory of the Anglo male and reserve themselves to be valuable social wombs in the creation of a new Texas society.

In this dichotomy, the Texas creation mythology is similar to much mythology based on Judeo-Christian and Greek ideologies. Jamake Highwater, exploring the prototypes Eve and Virgin Mary, found Eve to be the symbol of subordination as well as sexual overindulgence socially awarded women, whereas the Virgin Mary symbolizes woman's absolution of sin if she appears as sexually abstinent. Highwater declares that women are still perceived as "inferior creatures torn between the innocence of Mary and the lustful willfulness of Eve" (Highwater 1990:23). According to this depiction, women who refuse to control their sexuality and who tempt men to abandon reason for sexual pleasure threaten men's rationality and the very foundation of civilization (Highwater 1990:92–93).

In these mythologies, a woman can either disrupt order and bring chaos or she can hold her proper, subordinate position by denying her sexuality. When she is a temptress, woman brings carnal knowledge to man and his subsequent fall from grace. When she keeps her sexuality in check, using her sexual power only according to man's directions, she is virtuous and deserving of man's protection and a place in proper society.

The perception of woman's innate chaotic "nature" has persisted, and it was particularly strong in the nineteenth century when the narratives of the Texas Revolution began to form. As Highwater notes, female sexuality was an enigma to nineteenth-century men— the "dark continent" in Sigmund Freud's terms (Highwater 1990:7). The unknownness of enigmas grants them power, for not only does the ordinary mortal not know the extent of that entity's power, but he also does not know how to control that power once it is manifest. According to this ideology, only extraordinary males can control the power of female sexuality.

In the Texas creation mythology, only the Anglo men can control women; they alone have the power of women at their disposal. Mythologically, the Anglo male can distinguish the Eves from the Marys, and they alone know how to deal with each type of woman. In battle the Anglo male denies the tempting, defends the virtuous, and embraces the technological. In contrast, the quintessential Mexican male in the mythology, Santa Anna, is unable to control his sexuality and consequently falls prey to Eve's protégées.

Santa Anna, by having a sexual relationship with a woman, is diminished in various ways. His energy has been consumed by Emily Morgan, who has "bedwhipped" him into a physically and mentally fatigued state. The belief that sexual activity diminishes men stems from a nineteenth-century concept of man as a machine with a limited supply of energy. Highwater explains the consequences for men investing their limited energy on sexual activities:

> [I]t was widely believed that men should refrain from sexual activity before events that called upon their best efforts: business transactions, sporting activities, military confrontations, and political decisions. In this way, an unusual attitude found its way into society: an occult notion, not unlike vampirism, that envisioned women as depleting, stealing, and confiscating the life force of men.
>
> (Highwater 1990:162)

Santa Anna, in the creation myth, spends himself on sexual pleasure, foolishly allowing Emily to consume his energy, rather than wisely saving himself for his military pursuits. His sexual nature overrides his business sense, and thus he loses Texas.

It is important to note who, among the men and women of the Texas creation mythology, is allotted the role of nature and sexuality, that is, who receives the role of Eve, Adam, Christ, or Mary. According to this legend, the temptress, Emily Morgan, is a mulatto, a term which suggests an in-between category, being neither Black nor Anglo. Emily Morgan is, according to the mythology, the product of a relationship between a Black woman and an Anglo man. Although springing from a private "bedroom integration," she embodies the southern ideal of Anglo plantation owners and Black slaves combining for profit in the South. This combination, within the mythology, spells the end of Hispanic rule in Texas. The "cultured" southern Anglo male, with the help of his "nature-oriented" slaves, is able to settle and make productive this wilderness.

Implicitly, the beauty of Emily Morgan derives from her "tan-skinned" appearance, a result of her Anglo-Black parentage. The implication is that a Black woman would not have caught Santa Anna's eye. Born of Anglo imagination, the legendary Emily Morgan is able to derail Santa Anna from his goal via her Anglo-derived beauty.

But giving Emily the supposedly more attractive skin tone is not the only reason for assigning her an Anglo-Black origin. Another, implied reason is that she must be at least half Black because, supposedly, Anglo women will not have sexual relations with Hispanic men. According to the mythology, Anglo women will not even *consider* such relationships. A temptress willing to bed down with Santa Anna must be of another ethnicity with questionable virtue.

Furthermore, these temptresses can be bought. Emily Morgan's status as a slave is essential here. This mythological product of Anglo culture's private integration with Black nature is for sale along with all her services, as is apparent in McAlister's and Shuffler's proposed monuments.

Emily's renown as the "Yellow Rose of Texas" also reveals her in-between status of being neither fully Black nor fully Anglo; that is, Emily is neither fully a creature of nature nor fully a cultured being. "Yellow Rose" denotes the natural fertility of a flower. But Emily is not a wildflower; she is a cultured rose. Mythologically born from the union of a refined southern man and an earthy slave woman, she is raised by someone (owner) in an enclosed area (slavery = garden). Santa Anna plucks the rose from its rightful owner as he passes by the "garden" (Morgan's plantation).

This theft will, according to the legend, ultimately bring his downfall. Santa Anna, being aligned with nature, has no right to the cultured products of the southern Anglo man. Although Santa Anna tries desperately to appear as one of the cultured human beings, he is unable to maintain his cultural facade, and his true "nature" comes out. By destroying his ability to function militarily, Emily exposes his unrefined nature under the trappings of European culture.[1] Although Santa Anna has paraded through Texas in foreign finery, he runs from the battlefield stripped to his underwear. He ends up wearing old clothes he finds in a barn, further connecting him with nature via animals.

According to the mythology, Santa Anna ignores the path of reason known to cultural beings; he follows instead the call of the gonads. According to the legend, Santa Anna is so sexually oriented that he makes exceedingly poor transactions; he trades a million square miles of northern Mexico for a few hours of sexual pleasure.[2] All three of the most popular versions of the Emily Morgan legend—Shuffler's, Turner's, and McAlister's—stress this point. Santa

Anna, by trading Texas for sexual pleasure, is "by nature" an extremely poor businessman.

The total ineptitude awarded Santa Anna in the narratives about the Battle of San Jacinto stems from his tryst with Emily, who is sexually consuming him. Santa Anna loses himself (his energy) to this woman, violating the nineteenth-century understanding of the importance of conserving sperm. Ben Barker-Benfield explores the nineteenth-century beliefs regarding the consequences of sperm loss, as spelled out in *The Student's Manual*, an extremely popular book by an American minister, Rev. John Todd:

"Energy" . . . was construed as sexual. The memory was "debilitated," the mind "deteriorated and weakened" by masturbation because sperm was believed to be "the concentrated powers of [man's] perfected being. . . ." "Sperm is the purest extract from the blood, and according to the expression of Feruel, *totus homo semen est.*" This was the ancient belief that blood was life, and that life's transmission fluid, sperm, was the sum and representation of its bearer. . . . Warnings of physical excess in copulation went hand in hand with warning [*sic*] about masturbation. "Runts," feeble infants and girls would be produced by debilitated sperm, old man's prostrated sperm, businessman's tired sperm, masturbator's exhausted, debaucher's exceeded, contraceptor's impeded, coward's unpatriotic, and newlywed's green, sperm.

(Barker-Benfield 1974:49–50)

By nineteenth-century science, Santa Anna, because of his purported sexual engagements, does not stand a chance on the battlefield. His depleted "energy" supply leaves him utterly debilitated and confused.

Sam Houston, by contrast, has his business sense about him at the end of the battle. Instead of spending himself on biological women in the midst of battle, he has spent his time with the Twin Sisters cannon. When he finds himself the victor at San Jacinto, Houston continues to act in a rational manner. Although he is enraged at the atrocities committed by Santa Anna, he understands that this Mexican general is worth more to him alive than dead, and he therefore restrains himself from committing any emotionally motivated acts of vengeance. Sam Houston's debilitation comes from a battle wound, not from a low sperm count. According to the narratives, his mind is functioning perfectly well at the end of the battle.

The nineteenth-century belief that sexual activity drains men continues in the last part of the twentieth century, as is apparent from McAlister's depiction of Santa Anna as "bedwhipped." In contrast, the abstinent Anglos are extremely productive. They get a high score in the number of Mexicans they kill at each battle.

Not only is Santa Anna's energy level down; the "energy" he has is defective as well. Santa Anna's sperm, when considered in *The Student's Manual* terms, is deficient on several grounds. So defective is his sperm that no children will come from Santa Anna's union with Emily; at least, we do not hear of any resulting children. By contrast, Emily's progenitor, an Anglo male, must have had more vigorous, productive sperm, which he spent on producing another piece of property.[3]

The comparison of Sam Houston to Santa Anna in the mythology questions the propriety of what each man—and, by extension, each group—is doing during the middle of the day. Houston is ready for the business of battle; he and his army plan on being as productive as possible, whereas the Mexican soldiers are dallying with women or sleeping. In the accounts of the San Jacinto battle, the Mexican soldiers are so militarily inept that the Texans are able to come to within two hundred yards before being noticed, a point which is often stressed in the narratives.[4] The ultimate atrocity in the middle of the day, however, is Santa Anna's sexual indulgence.

The issue of what type of services Emily renders is not questioned in any of the versions of the legend; what *is* a point of departure in at least one other written version of the legend is Emily's motives for having sexual relations with Santa Anna. In the version written by Martha Anne Turner, Emily Morgan is "captured" by Santa Anna, that is, taken against her will. Turner's version claims that Emily Morgan survived the battle and returned to Morgan's plantation; Morgan granted Emily her freedom for her part in the Battle of San Jacinto. According to Turner, Morgan later bought Emily a home in a community of free Negroes in the Houston area. On the issue of "willingness," Turner denies Emily's interest in Santa Anna:

> Was the lovely mulatto infatuated with the Emperor of Mexico? Despite any hypothetical attraction she might have felt for Santa Anna, Emily Morgan was a captive and was familiar with the status quo. Increasingly, the belief that she performed her service for her adopted home of Texas out of loyalty is gaining credence.

(Turner 1981:28)

Emily, by using her sexuality in the service of her proper master (the Anglo male), aids her "adopted home" of Texas and therefore is granted a home of her own in what the author finds an appropriate (i.e., "free Negro") community.

With the different endings for the Emily Morgan story, we have two possible avenues for a female mulatto slave in conjunction with a Hispanic male: (1) She can enjoy the relationship and any possible status transformation that may accompany it; or (2) she can be a good, loyal servant who respects the status quo. The endings of the stories depend on her choice (as well as on whether the writer is male or female). When she ignores the status quo, we lose track of her, left with the impression that she may have been killed in the melee; her life becomes negligible. But in respecting and preserving the status quo, she is rewarded.

Preserving the status quo is, after all, the primary function of mythology, as one prominent anthropologist points out: "[T]he aim of mythology is to ensure that as closely as possible . . . the future will remain faithful to the present and to the past" (Lévi-Strauss 1978:43). Although Claude Lévi-Strauss is speaking in this statement of societies without writing or archives, the words hold true for societies with written accounts of the popular histories, especially societies that revere movies and other public media. This quality is particularly apparent in the Texas creation mythology, whose framework reveals the defined social categories. The social boundaries of the mythology must be maintained if Texas society is to continue unchanged, with a subordinate status assigned to ethnic groups other than Anglos and to women in relation to men.

This subordinate status accounts, in part, for the little public acclaim awarded women and Tejano defenders at the Alamo and San Jacinto in comparison to the recognition given Anglo men. This "unspoken" quality of these lesser heroes is clear in the case of Emily Morgan. In all three versions of the Emily Morgan legend cited above, Emily wittingly contributes to Santa Anna's downfall. She is thus a partner in his defeat and in Houston's victory. But her legend is rarely included in the written versions of the Texas creation myth, and her name is never part of the public ceremonies occurring outside or inside the Alamo. Emily Morgan, as a slave, is the silent partner in the winning of Texas.

The most public recognition of the Emily Morgan character is a high-rise hotel bordering the Alamo grounds, the Emily Morgan Hotel, which gives her character a silent but imposing presence on Alamo Plaza. A plaque in the lobby describes Emily Morgan's role in the winning of Texas: " . . . Were it not for the heroics of the beautiful mulatto slave Emily Morgan, Texas may to this day have remained Coahuilla y Texas, Republic of Mexico. . . . Santa Anna's eye for women and Emily Morgan's allegiance to Texas proved to be a fatal combination for Mexico."

Although Emily Morgan is not celebrated in front of the Alamo at any time during the year, she is the focus of an annual gathering at the San Jacinto Monument outside of Houston: On the eve of San Jacinto Day, a group of local lawyers and judges who have formed the club SKYRT (Secret Knights of the Yellow Rose of Texas) hold an overnight party on the grounds surrounding the San Jacinto Monument. After consuming much beer, they invoke the spirit of Emily Morgan (Henson 1990). She is goddess of the raucous rather than the divine, uplifting the SKYRT all night long.

In the Texas creation mythology, Emily Morgan, being a sexy mulatto slave, is at the disposal of any man. This categorical distinction of who will appear in which roles continues in the mythology with the figure of Melchora Barrera, a seventeen-year-old Mexican woman living in San Antonio at the time of the 1836 Alamo siege. The *documented* Melchora was the daughter of a Mexican army officer. Her father died prior to the Alamo siege, and Melchora remained in San Antonio with her mother. According to the writings of one of Santa Anna's officers, Santa Anna, upon arriving in San Antonio and hearing of the young and beautiful Melchora, desired her as a concubine (he was already married). But her mother refused to let Santa Anna have Melchora except through marriage. Santa Anna arranged a fake wedding to persuade her mother of his good intentions. With one of Santa Anna's officers playing the role of a priest for the phony wedding, Santa Anna "married" Melchora during his siege of the Alamo (Tinkle 1958: 105–106).

In most accounts, Melchora and her mother simply appear as innocent dupes to a corrupt and lecherous Mexican general and his cronies. But George McAlister, in his tale of the Alamo heroes' lives and loves, takes the Melchora figure and fabricates situations and events to allow the historic Melchora the needed characteristics to fit into the mythologized social categories. In McAlister's version, Melchora is the product of a sexual union between an Anglo man and a Mexican woman (apparently another instance of "bedroom integration" in the author's eyes). She is the parallel of Emily Morgan, being pure sexuality, and therefore is fair game for all. McAlister allows Travis time with Melchora before Santa Anna arrives:

She had the loveliest cream-colored complexion . . . , but . . . it was only the topping of a figure that actually embarrassed Will

[Travis]. He could hardly look into her twinkling brown eyes without dropping his own to view her perfectly formed breasts displayed magnificently by a low-cut elegant gown . . . [with] openings in just the right places.

$\qquad$ (McAlister 1988b:101)

Once again, skin tone is important in the mythology: Melchora must have the lighter skin given by an Anglo father, so that she is beautiful enough, in McAlister's eyes, to attract the ultimate Anglo male, Travis. But this new creation retains the animal nature allotted the Mexican culture in her extreme sexuality. Melchora is definitely the aggressor in her relationship with Travis, forcing the poor, embarrassed man to drop his eyes and look at her breasts.

McAlister makes his Melchora desperately in love with Travis; at the fandango, she pulls Travis down into the shadows, "her body hot with pulse and passion" (McAlister 1988b:169). Fortunately, the reader is spared what might have followed by a courier who interrupts the fandango with news of Santa Anna's approach. When the time comes for the Texans to fortify themselves inside the old mission, McAlister has Travis walk toward the Alamo, with Melchora screaming that he is a fool walking into his coffin; she pleads with him to run away with her.

McAlister's Travis, however, resists the unmanning seductivity of such sexual beings. He chooses to fight for Texas, which he professes to "love" (McAlister 1988b:172). The image of Travis is that of an intelligent and honorable man, investing his time, love, and energy in real estate, as opposed to Santa Anna who falls prey to his own animal nature and consequently loses Texas.

But prior to the time for transformation to martial hero, Travis has human interests. As is apparent in McAlister's story of the relationship between Travis and Melchora, Anglo male–Hispanic female sexual relationships are acceptable in the mythology. Such relationships are a source of entertainment, but not usually of marriage.

This point becomes particularly clear in a scene appearing in the uncut version of the 1988 IMAX film *Alamo . . . The Price of Freedom*. In this scene, a fictitious seventeen-year-old Mexican girl named Rosita is being detained by an amorous Tennessee volunteer in the bell tower of San Fernando Cathedral the day Santa Anna's army arrives in San Antonio.[5] When the uncut version of the film was previewed by Hispanic community leaders, several of these leaders were incensed over the scene in the bell tower, and they began a public outcry against the film as demeaning to Hispanics. A

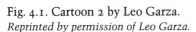

Fig. 4.1. Cartoon 2 by Leo Garza.
*Reprinted by permission of Leo Garza.*

local political cartoonist focused on the social categories present within the scene and the protest surrounding it (Fig. 4.1).[6]

As Leo Garza makes clear in his cartoon, any sexual relationships between Hispanic men and Anglo women are, according to the mythology, possible only through force; purportedly, Anglo women recoil at the thought of being sexually involved with Hispanic men. Hispanic women, however, are supposed to welcome such relationships with Anglo men. For his part, the Anglo man sees the sexual interlude as filling in dead time while he is waiting for more significant life events, such as becoming a military hero.

What does happen in the mythology to Hispanic men who seek sexual relationships with Anglo women? There exists at least one account of such an attempt, a fictional narrative by Richard Buckley, published in the *San Antonio Express* in 1911. In this narrative, Santos Cordona, a lieutenant in the Mexican army, falls in love with Ruth Burgess, a young and beautiful Anglo woman with golden hair and blue eyes. In 1835, Burgess and her father find Cordona among the dead and wounded Mexican soldiers of an October 28 battle near the Mission Concepcion. Out of humaneness, Ruth nurses Cordona back to health. He returns to Mexico, only to come back to Texas as part of Santa Anna's march on the Alamo.

Although sent on a scouting mission by Santa Anna, Cordona turns his "staunch little Spanish horse" toward the Burgess home. Cordona, dressed in the clothes of a ranchero, goes to profess his love to Ruth. Upon his arrival, he finds Ruth in mourning for her father who has recently died. With "Latin-Aztec impetuosity," he seizes the opportunity and begs Ruth to allow him to be her protector. In response to this advance, she makes "a shrinking gesture," which goes unheeded by the passionate Cordona. He continues to elaborate on how much he loves her and how he can provide for her. Finally, she interrupts him, declaring that his avowal of love grieves her. She explains that she is betrothed to a Tennessean, Ross Kemble, who is inside the Alamo fortress. At this news Cordona "clutch[es] the crown of the large sombrero he h[olds] in his lap, convulsively. His lustrous black eyes gr[ow] big with a momentary look of triumph." He realizes that Ross Kemble and the other Texans will soon be overtaken by Santa Anna's army. But then another emotion awakens in Cordona, that of pity for the weeping Ruth.

The author of the legend hypothesizes what is running through Cordona's mind as he mentally processes the possibilities: "Psychologists might well tell us if they do not, that one passion when brought into conflict with another often serves to interpret its fellow with startling distinctness." Cordona apparently chooses the right path through the emotional maze. In a pensive ride after leaving Ruth, the proper actions for him to take become clear in his mind, and he thanks God for having shown him the proper course. He returns to Ruth's home and tells her that should her beloved come to visit her, she must not allow him to return to the Alamo. Cordona then goes to the Alamo fortress, still dressed as a ranchero, and manages to get a message to Ross Kemble that his fiancée Ruth Burgess is extremely ill. Kemble leaves, and Cordona takes his place inside the Alamo. Cordona is killed in Santa Anna's assault.

The tale has Cordona die beside James Bowie. Perhaps the message is that death is the fate of anyone, even an Anglo man, who marries across social categories. Or perhaps the proximity of these men simply serves to raise Santos Cordona to the position of hero, who, in respecting and defending the status quo (in choosing the proper path), joins the ranks of honorable men. Whatever the significance, he still may not have a sexual relationship with an Anglo woman.

Lest the reader mistake this story as simply unrequited love, the author makes clear near the beginning of the tale the impropriety of Cordona's affection for this Anglo woman:

He was in the thrall of a fascinating image that had haunted him like a vision of Paradise since he left these parts three months before. He knew that he did wrong to entertain this vision. He felt that he had no right to indulge the wild, tormenting dream of winning the hand of the fair-haired daughter of an alien race, against which his country was now waging a merciless war. . . .

Yet, what ardent swain is there who may philosophize with love, or be daunted by the minor scruples of conscience? Certainly not Santos Cordona, in whose veins flowed the hot blood of Castile and Mexico.

(Buckley 1911:87)

This passage foreshadows Cordona's doom, for he knows he is wrong to dream of marrying Ruth; "swains" have no business with the angelic beings of Paradise. Receiving direction from above, Cordona realizes his mistake; he decides to die and allow the proper union to take place. He, as the old order of Mexico, accepts his defeat and dies so that the new order as embodied in Ruth Burgess and Ross Kemble can begin.

The author of the Santos Cordona legend makes clear his belief that Mexican males are innately sexual beings: It's in the blood. Sexuality flows through these men, interrupting their ability to reason and to understand that they are, by natural design, swains. In this perspective, the Mexican people cannot be anything but peasants and creatures of nature, no matter what cultural facades they offer.

In the Texas creation mythology, the archetype of these sexual beings is, of course, Santa Anna. Santa Anna pretends to be a cultural being; but in his love of fine clothing and food, he becomes excessive, rotting culture (European culture) that, in its decomposing state, is as undesirable as primitive nature.[7] In the mythology, Santa Anna's sexual encounters with women strip away his cultural veneer and reveal his true inner being.

Being so ruled by his sexuality, Santa Anna even goes after Anglo women, ignoring his naturally lower status: in the mythology, Santa Anna attempts to claim, after the Alamo battle, Susanna Dickinson and her infant daughter, Angelina. According to the story line, Susanna, the just-widowed wife of a captain in the Texas force, survives the storming of the Alamo with Angelina, and shortly after the battle, she is brought before Santa Anna. Santa Anna orders that the infant be handed to him, and he places the child on his knee. He then turns on the charm, attempting to persuade the beautiful, black-haired Susanna that he is a kind, providing man that will treat these two Anglo beauties lovingly. He pets Angelina, and tells Susanna that Angelina is too pretty to be raised in such a place as Texas and that Susanna should allow him to take both Angelina and her to Mexico City to live.

Full of anger and grief, Susanna steadfastly refuses Santa Anna's proposals, declaring that Texas is Angelina's home. Susanna knows not to submit to this Mexican man. She rejects the relative security of the Mexican army, choosing to walk east to Sam Houston and the remainder of the Texas army (cf. Jakes 1986, McAlister 1988b, Tolbert 1959, Tinkle 1958). Having failed to entice Susanna, Santa Anna will, according to the story line, acquire Emily Morgan's services.

In the mythology, Santa Anna is both pure sexuality and thus military incompetence; in contrast, the Alamo defenders and Susanna Dickinson are asexuality and military expertise. The incompetence versus expertise appears in the number of Mexican soldiers killed in the assault at the Alamo, and in the later Texan victory at San Jacinto; the sexual versus asexual appears in the encounter between Santa Anna and Susanna. In legends involving Santa Anna and other Hispanics, sexuality is accented, whereas the Anglo characters within these legends are relatively asexual beings. Susanna, rather than being "a gal on the make," is a matronly figure (albeit a beautiful one). In similar mode, Ruth Burgess is the loving daughter and faithful fiancée. Both women react negatively to the idea of sexual relationships with Hispanic men; both represent the relatively asexual Virgin Mary option of the Judeo-Christian dichotomy.

The sexual abstinence extends to Anglo males in their relationships with all biological women during battles. The most visible Anglo male with potential for sexual relationships within this mythology is Travis, most often portrayed as being young, handsome, and well educated. He enters the Texas Revolution, according to legend, engaged to an Anglo woman, Rebecca Cummings, whose cat's-eye ring he wears. Although he is involved in the proper relationship for an Anglo man and an Anglo woman, Travis, as the archetypal Anglo male, will not consummate his relationship with Rebecca. Travis will not spend himself on biological women, but rather saves himself and his seed for Texas and the Alamo.

Travis's image within the mythology derives primarily from the Son figure of the Christian Trinity, but it also derives from a nineteenth-century fascination with the romantic, chivalrous knight. With the resurgence of chivalry developing in the Romantic period of literature and continuing into the twentieth century, chastity and death (along with the preservation of sperm) become goals in themselves. The sacrificial victim and the romantic lover/hero images merge in this ideology, with chastity as man's triumph over nature. Death allows romantic love to remain forever chaste, and thus death is both an obstruction to and object of such lovers (Highwater 1990:133, 135).

The death of Travis at a young age and the sacrificial tone of the creation mythology fit perfectly the mold of a romantic, chivalrous death. As the archetypal Anglo male, Travis rises above his animal nature and embraces the most noble love in the act of denying himself the sexual gratification and potential children promised in his engagement to Rebecca. In leaving his relationship with Rebecca unconsummated (in the mythology), he spends his energy on defending Texas; he dies, with a full sperm count, on the battlefield.

The 1988 IMAX film is the version of the Alamo battle that best portrays Travis's romantic aptitude within the Texas creation myth. One scene within the film is particularly revealing: On the final night of the siege, after Travis and his men have already made their decision to stay within the Alamo and die fighting, Travis retires to the room that has served as his headquarters throughout the siege. He looks at the cat's-eye ring on his finger, and hears the voice of Rebecca telling him of her love. A child's voice enters in, saying, "I love you, Father." He removes the ring from his finger, threads a string through it, and walks to the room where Susanna cares for infant Angelina. He places the ring necklace over Angelina's head, saying, "I'd like her to have this. I don't think I'll be needing it" (cf. also McAlister 1988a:177–178).

In handing the ring to Angelina, Travis passes his right to family and future to the only Anglo child within the Alamo compound. It is her duty in life to be a womb bearing the new Texas society; Travis is the fate-ordained sacrifice who dies so that society as embodied in Angelina may live. His gift of the ring represents the passing of reproduction from Travis and his generation to Angelina and her generation. The gift makes explicit the role of Anglo women within this new Texan society: Anglo men bring technological productivity and sacrifice; Anglo women bring social reproductivity.

These social wombs are the asexual women idealized during the nineteenth century.[8] Travis's act of passing the ring to a prepubescent female emphasizes the asexuality of the Anglo women involved in the Texas creation mythology. Although a promise of conjugal happiness lies in Rebecca's gift of the ring to Travis, no sexual innuendos surround Travis's gift to infant Angelina.

Within the Texas creation myth, the asexuality of the Anglo women stands in contrast to the sexuality of ethnic women. So extreme is the sexuality of such women as Emily Morgan that her union with Santa Anna, rather than being reproductive, is diminishing. Furthermore, Santa Anna and Emily Morgan subvert sex as reproduction by making it an economic transaction; according to the three versions cited above, Santa Anna "pays" for his time with Emily with "approximately a million square miles of the American West." Thus sex moves out of the private domain of family into the public domain of economics. In this transformation, the sexual act loses its fertility. Prostitutes are sexual organs, not reproductive wombs. In the mythology, Anglo women are the valuable social wombs and women of other ethnicities are the prostitutes.

*It is important to note here the extent to which the mythology is an inversion of archival records.* According to historical documents, the women who turn to prostitution are Susanna Dickinson and Angelina, *not* Emily Morgan. Both Susanna and Angelina are left destitute after the Texas Revolution, despite Susanna's pleas for financial help from the Texas government. Alamo historian Jeff Long depicts Susanna as "a virtual model of self-destruction" who must resort to prostitution for survival after the Alamo battle. When she becomes a young woman, Angelina also turns to prostitution, and dies at a young age of a hemorrhaging uterus (Long 1990: 339).

In light of their later lives, it is no wonder most narratives of Susanna and Angelina stop shortly after the Alamo battle. Even when their fate is discussed publicly, it is often done in an obscure manner. In a speech made to the House of Representatives in 1852, Guy Bryan describes the fate of Angelina thus: "She failed to secure the education which she craved and later died in Galveston after a life of drifting, over which history has drawn a kindly veil" (reprinted in *San Antonio Express News*, May 10, 1918).

Personified history, in drawing such veils, complements the ideology of the people reciting the narratives. History unpersonified is much less gracious to the categories of the Texas creation mythology. What does the public record say about the person behind the Emily Morgan character? Historian Margaret Henson, researching Emily, rejects almost every favored detail of the legend:

Few Texas tales are as full of distortions as that of the fabled "Yellow Rose," or Emily Morgan. In fact, she was not a slave, her last name was not Morgan, and the myth that she delayed Santa Anna in his tent is just that, myth. Nor is there any evidence to connect Emily with the popular 19th century ballad, "The Yellow Rose of Texas."

(Henson 1986: 60)

The flesh-and-bone person behind the legend, Emily West, was a *free Black* woman living in Texas at the time of the Texas Revolution. She was captured by the Mexican army on its march east, but she managed to escape during the Battle of San Jacinto. As Henson points out, there is no evidence to suggest that she was ever in Santa Anna's tent, much less involved with him sexually: "Even eyewitnesses who had every reason to criticize the Mexican dictator fail to mention his dallying with a woman" (Henson 1986:60).

But a free Black woman living in Texas does not match the prototype supported by the Texas creation mythology. The mythology must have the categories respected, and thus emerges the character Emily Morgan. Via the mythology, Emily West loses her name, ethnic status, and freedom. In their stead, she receives characteristics that support the status quo ideology: She becomes an Anglo-produced piece of property to be used to the Texans' advantage.

Under the documentation light, the figures of Emily Morgan and Susanna and Angelina Dickinson become inverted. The figure of Travis does a similar reversal under such scrutiny. William B. Travis may have attempted a chivalrous image with his use of a sword and fiery retorts to demands for surrender. But when the historical haze allowed in the IMAX movie (and many of the written narratives) clears, a different image of Travis emerges. Although Travis left his wife in South Carolina pregnant with a second child, he listed himself as a widower upon his arrival in Texas. And far from maintaining a chaste life in accord with the Romantic code, Travis became sexually involved with more than fifty women during his few years in Texas, at least according to his diary entries. Historian Jeff Long points out that Travis noted his sexual exploits at the end of his entries in crude Spanish, listing what number the woman ranked in his sexual life, and using the verb *chingar* to describe the sexual act, a word which denotes degradation. Furthermore, Travis had a severe case of venereal disease, and he recorded its flare-up in his diary as well. According to Jeff Long, Travis transmitted the disease to his fiancée Rebecca Cummings (Long 1990:34–35).

This past denies the chaste, sacrificial-victim role assigned to Travis within the mythology. The Travis who leads the men of the Alamo garrison to martyrdom in asking them to cross his line furrowed in the Alamo dirt must not, in the popularized versions, contain these flaws of "nature." Although some of the narratives do mention the mystery surrounding Travis's life prior to the Alamo siege, and a few remark on the purported hotheadedness of Travis, almost all depictions of Travis allow him the transformation necessary to be the heroic victim whose sacrifice brings life to Texas. Any unheroic motives and attributes are filtered out in this transformation from individual life to historic communal figure.[9] The creation mythology needs this figure of the Christian Trinity, and William B. Travis becomes who he must be to fill the role.

The entire trinity—Travis, Bowie, and Crockett—receive this transformation. In the narratives, past sins are either ignored or forgiven in the final acts of sacrifice in the Alamo. During this time, these figures appear as the ideal Anglos, focusing their energies on sacrifice (killing and being killed) and spirituality rather than bodily pleasures. They conserve their "energy" for use in their encounters with other men and in creating Texas. Even the least positive depiction of Travis—the arrogant and egotistical foil to John Wayne's Crockett—does not allow Travis to be the sexually consumed and diseased man his diary reveals him to be. The commander of the Alamo must follow the ideal of asexuality when in the limelight. Before battle he must follow the designs of Christ and of the chivalrous cavalier if the Alamo sacrifice is to bear new life. He must embody the spirit of sacrifice and leave in his death an empty tomb.

# Chapter 5. Heroic Kings and Wealthy Queens

The Texas creation mythology focuses on the birth of Texas from the death of heroes. From the Alamo—the archetypal social womb—springs the "majestic matron," Texas, who is "the Queen of Plenty, the Mother of Heroes."[1] The Alamo, thus, represents life more than it represents death. In the mythology, the Alamo contains the needed fertility to serve as womb for the new Texas society.

The Alamo currently serves as womb in reproducing a localized version of Texas society as embodied in the Texas Cavaliers (the "heroes") and in the Queen of the Order of the Alamo and her duchesses, selected by the elite group of men who constitute the Order of the Alamo (possessors of "plenty"). Annually the Texas Cavaliers and the Order of the Alamo hold their individual secret meetings inside the walls of the Alamo to produce (1) the new Queen of the Order of the Alamo and (2) the new defenders of Texas heritage, the Texas Cavalier initiates, from whom will someday arise the new king to reign during Fiesta San Antonio. The ceremonies surrounding these royal figures' ascension to Fiesta thrones declare who may use the Alamo for reproduction and the significance of the Texas creation mythology in perpetuating Texas society as envisioned by these groups.

The Texas Cavaliers organization is purportedly one of the three most prestigious all-male clubs in San Antonio. In his study of the Texas Cavaliers, Tom Walker ranks this organization third in prestige behind the Order of the Alamo, whose membership is composed primarily of men of leisure, and the German Club, whose membership is of civically prominent men. In contrast, Texas Cavaliers members are more likely to be of the mercantile class "who, though from prominent families, actually work for a living: bourgeois aristocrats, with the accent on 'bourgeois'" (Walker 1983:215). Whereas the members of the Order of the Alamo *generally* represent the old-money families in San Antonio, some Texas Cavaliers represent recent, new-money arrivals to San Antonio society.

The Texas Cavaliers' constitution requires that a potential new member be a resident of Bexar County for two continuous years. Once a man has been selected as a Cavalier, his sons have a good chance of being accepted as well when they come of age (twenty-five years old). Walker notes that every year about seventy names are submitted by Texas Cavaliers as potential new members. About two-thirds of the men nominated for membership are sons and sons-in-law of Cavaliers. Out of these nominees, the twenty-four who have received recommendations by the entire club are submitted to the Cavaliers' board of directors, who choose not more than twelve to join the Cavaliers that year.

Family connections are, according to Walker, of the highest importance in selecting new members of this club as well as those of the German Club and the Order of the Alamo: "An ambitious woman can marry a Cavalier or a prospective Cavalier and look forward to not only a career in San Antonio society but also progeny who may become Fiesta royalty" (Walker 1983:216). The Texas Cavalier organization forms a stepping-stone to the other two; its members can conceivably have children who will become part of the in-town Fiesta royalty in the Order of the Alamo coronation, comprising the most socially prominent young women in San Antonio and chosen almost exclusively from the relatives of members of the Order of the Alamo and the German Club.[2]

Thus the Cavaliers' role and position is one of intermediary in classes within San Antonio society; the Cavaliers mediate between the working class and the men of leisure. They also mediate between the militia and civilians. But their intermediary role is not only between groups of people; they also serve as mediators between the past and the present, with their chivalrous image and modern uniform.

In his history of the Texas Cavaliers, Henry Graham, himself a Texas Cavalier, outlines the several objectives the founder, John Carrington, had for the organization. The foremost of these was the continuance of horsemanship in the industrialized, motorized world. But Carrington also wanted the Cavaliers to sponsor a pilgrimage to the Alamo to honor the Alamo heroes, to sponsor a Fiesta King, and to form a link between the civilian and military sectors of San Antonio (Graham 1976:11). The original purpose statement of the Texas Cavaliers reinforces Graham's contention about horsemanship being the primary reason for founding the group, especially when juxtaposed to the revised purpose statement that appeared in 1946:

> [original] The purpose of this organization shall be to encourage horsemanship and to pay homage to the memory of the heroes of the Alamo.
>
> [revised] This organization is a non-profit association, created and existing to honor the memory of the matchless heroes who fell at the Alamo and whose blazing pyres lighted the way to victory and independence at San Jacinto; to keep green in the minds of people, near and far, the glorious, glamorous history of Texas and the part San Antonio played in it; to encourage interest in horsemanship and other attributes and features of Texas tradition and pioneer life; to celebrate many decades of peace with neighboring nations; and to commemorate on the banks of the San Antonio River, the joy and sorrow—the triumph and sacrifice—which that graceful stream has shared with the inhabitants of this area down through the centuries.

In the revised purpose statement the Texas Cavaliers have staked their claim to the two most-visited tourist attractions in San Antonio—the Alamo and the River Walk.[3] The Texas Cavaliers claim both as their rightful domain through paying homage at each during Fiesta.

In his history of the Texas Cavaliers, Graham notes that horsemanship has been diminished in importance and the San Antonio River emphasized primarily because the Texas Cavaliers were having difficulty obtaining horses as mounts in parades and they, as a group, were more interested in staking out the River Parade as their domain during Fiesta.

But Graham neglects to mention the Cavaliers' greatly extended reverence for the Alamo heroes and declared interest in preserving their memory, even on the San Antonio River. This river is the site of ribaldry during Fiesta—drinking, dining, dancing, and sleeping it all off in the high-rise hotels on its banks. The river represents tourist dollars and business within the San Antonio area and is thus an important focus for the businessman image of the Texas Cavaliers. The Alamo, in contrast, is Texans' most holy site, shrine and destination of the solemn pilgrimage to commemorate the Texas heroes of the 1836 battle. It is the legitimizing source in San Antonio for "traditional" groups, that is, those groups who claim to form part of the city's past, especially during Fiesta. In claiming both sites as their domain during Fiesta, the Texas Cavaliers appear in command of the hub of financial activity, the San Antonio River, but they focus their origins and *raison d'être* on the Alamo defenders, thus linking themselves with the city's past.

The Alamo offers imagery of heroic acts and people, and the Texas Cavaliers work to invoke this image for their members. Although John Carrington had prescribed knightly outfits and jousts for the group during its first years of existence, the members quickly abandoned these cumbersome costumes and events, wanting something more believable in their heroic imagery. The Texas Cavaliers eventually chose a military-style uniform that, according to one journalist, favored that of the French Foreign Legion. (The journalist's comment is now part of the Texas Cavaliers' oral history about their uniform.) The modern Cavalier uniform is horizon blue and scarlet, with a blue coat with winged lapels and a broad-crowned blue cap.

The Texas Cavaliers' primary means of forming believable ties of kinship and tradition to heroes of the past comes in the group's private ceremony within the Alamo and the public ceremony following it. These ceremonies are held on the first Saturday of Fiesta, before the Pilgrimage to the Alamo and the Texas Cavaliers River Parade on the following Monday.

Although the ceremony held inside the Alamo church is secret, a former King Antonio explained that the private ceremony is to honor the heroes of the Alamo and to recognize deceased members of the Texas Cavaliers. The explicit Texas Cavalier message to the public comes in the investiture of King Antonio immediately following the secret ceremony within the Alamo church. This ceremony, which is held on the state property immediately in front of the Alamo church, proclaims the origins of the Texas Cavaliers and allows them to enact what they see as the debt relationship they have with the heroes of the Alamo. This relationship validates the Texas Cavaliers' created ancestry in the birthing of Texas and gives them the right to hold a secret ceremony in this most sacred of Texas landmarks. This homage also gives them the right to name one of their members to "reign over Fiesta," an action which occurs outside the walls of the famed church.

During the Texas Cavaliers' secret ceremony inside the Alamo church, the public waits outside, facing the church. Guards keep the general public off the state-owned Alamo property, which has been prepared with a red-draped stage containing a podium and a red-upholstered chair, all part of the investiture arena. A red-draped table with a microphone for the announcer stands near the curb on the left-hand side of the state property. Across the street on the city property of Alamo Plaza, grandstands reserved for special guests face the Alamo. These stands are filled with families of the Texas Cavaliers, military officers and their spouses, and city officials, such as the mayor. "Pinning," the exchange of Fiesta pins, abounds in this stand as alliances are fortified and people decorated.[4] Even the military officers participate in pinning; Fiesta is the only time during the year that military personnel in San Antonio may wear nonmilitary medals. The rest of the audience crowds on either side of these seats, sits on the curb, and fans out into the more distant grandstands.

The 1991 investiture of King Antonio, occurring during the Fiesta centennial, typified the transforming quality of this annual ceremony. Henry Guerra served as announcer for this event, as he has for several years. He is, to many San Antonians, the voice of Fiesta: his voice calls role from inside the Alamo church during the Pilgrimage to the Alamo, and his voice announces the floats at the Battle of Flowers Parade and during the Texas Cavaliers' River Parade.

Guerra is a local businessman (owner of a large funeral home in the city) who makes an avocation of proclaiming San Antonio's past; he has served as chairman of the Bexar County Historical Commission, and he offers vignettes of Texas history during his short program on the local radio station WOAI. In the minds of many San Antonians, Guerra *is* San Antonio's past. In the investiture ceremony, he symbolizes the Hispanic past graciously welcoming the new Texas society.

For the 1991 ceremony Guerra sat at a table covered with red cloth to the left of the Long Barracks. With his deep, resonating voice and measured phrases, he announced the beginning of the ceremony and prepared the audience for the emergence of the Texas Cavaliers and the arrival of the new king, declaring that King Antonio of the previous Fiesta would crown the new king.

The doors of the Alamo then opened, and the Texas Cavaliers moved out into the early evening light. They had just paid tribute to the dead, and they emerged to perform their duties. The Texas Cavalier member serving as the Commander in the ceremony declared to the audience the Texas Cavaliers' intent to commemorate the Alamo heroes. A prayer followed shortly after this explanation, given by King Antonio LXVII, Stanton Bell, who reigned during the 1989 Fiesta:

Bless all who here serve, merciful Father, with the indomitable
will for justice and truth. . . . Help us to uphold our traditions
and to preserve our unit. . . . Give us that same sure and certain
faith and strength, even as those who are here within these sacred walls gave their all, that we may know that we have served
faithfully and well.

(1991 Investiture of King Antonio)

After the prayer, the Commander acknowledged the degree to which
the previous year's King Antonio had carried out his duties representing the Texas Cavaliers. King Antonio LXVIII then thanked the
rest of the Texas Cavaliers as he prepared to turn his kingdom over
to the new King Antonio:

King Antonio LXVIII: I would like to express my appreciation to
the membership for their cooperation in assisting and helping me
to carry out the Texas Cavaliers' purpose of keeping alive in the
minds of the people far and near the glorious heroic history of
Texas and the Alamo. For sixty-four years the mantle of responsibility for this noble purpose has been passed down each year by
naming a succeeding King Antonio from the ranks of the Texas
Cavaliers. I now request that the king-elect be brought forward
so this historic succession can be maintained.

(1991 Investiture of King Antonio)

As the Texas Cavaliers prepared for the arrival of their new king,
Guerra prepared the audience for what was approaching the Alamo
and what was occurring within the state-owned property:

Guerra: As the order is given to bring forth the new Fiesta King,
the United States army drill team from Fort Myer, Virginia,
appears as a twenty-one-gun salute in honor of the new king
is fired from within the Alamo walls. . . . Now comes, also from
Fort Myer, Virginia, the Old Guard Fife and Drum Corps . . .
escorting the new king of Fiesta. The new king of Fiesta!

(1991 Investiture of King Antonio)

From behind the Long Barracks museum, out of the audience's sight,
twenty-one *cannon* (not gun) shots were firing as the new king approached. The two military companies from Fort Myer, Virginia, approached separately, the drill team coming first, stopping in front of

the main stand to perform to the rhythm of their marching feet and
the tapping of their guns. Then came the Old Guard Fife and Drum
Corps playing music and wearing costumes associated with the time
of the American Revolution. The new king followed, riding in a
horse-drawn carriage. He wore the king's jacket, heavy with medals
and adorned with gold braid. On his shoulders was the king's cape,
blue on the outside and scarlet inside. Around his waist was the
king's belt, its scabbard empty as he had not yet received the sword
of office. The carriage stopped in front of the Alamo; the new king
stepped from his carriage and walked toward the shrine.

For his investiture, the new king placed his left hand on the Christian Bible as he took the vow of the Texas Cavaliers, after which he
received the king's objects of office: the saber and plumed hat. Then
the former king proclaimed the passing of his title to his heir. The
new king then proclaimed the status and place of the old king as
being among "the other most honored and respected past kings,"
thus completing the transference.

The first duty of King Antonio LXIX was to announce the names
of the new Texas Cavaliers and to welcome them into the organization, calling each of them by name. He then recited the "ideals and
purposes" to which these new heroes are bound:

> King Antonio LXIX: First among these is to honor the memory of
> the matchless heroes who fell at the Alamo. Next is our duty to
> keep alive in the minds of people near and far the glorious his-
> tory of Texas in which the Alamo is the most shining chapter.
>
> (1991 Investiture of King Antonio)

The new king then reviewed the history of Texas as represented in
the six flags that "belong" to it. As the new king announced each
flag, the bearer brought it forward from behind the stage area to the
curb in front of the Alamo. The flags lined up according to the dia-
gram below:

Alamo

Texas   Confederate   United States        Mexico   France   Spain

Thus the Texas, Confederate, and United States flags were on the
right side of the Alamo, left side of the audience; and the flags of
Mexico, France, and Spain were on the left side of the Alamo, right
side of the audience. Later in the ceremony, when the new king requested that the flag of the Texas Cavaliers and the flag of Fiesta be

brought forward, the Texas Cavalier flag was carried over to the side of the Alamo with the flags of Texas, the Confederacy, and the United States; the Fiesta flag was carried to the other.

After the presentation of these flags, the new king announced the lighting of the memorial flame:

> King Antonio LXIX: Tonight we will light a flame before the Alamo in grateful remembrance. Like the lives of these heroes, it will burn briefly, but will shine always in our memories.

> (1991 Investiture of King Antonio)

The new king carried a lighted torch to a footed basin standing near the curb in front of the Alamo and lit the fuel in the basin. King Antonio LXIX was then welcomed by the citizenry of San Antonio as represented in the mayor, Lila Cockrell, who offered him the key to the city. Thus it appeared that both the military and the civilian sectors of San Antonio declared the legitimacy of this temporary king. They witnessed his ascension to the throne and declared him as their king, granting him authority to reign during Fiesta.

In the mythology, the heroes' transcendence of death comes in the funeral pyre; similarly, the new Texas Cavaliers' rite of passage ends in the lighting of the memorial flame. The fire of each is connected, via mythology and ritual, to the honor of the fallen heroes. Each is declared eternal in the minds of the Texas Cavaliers, who proclaim as their duty the perpetuation of the heroes' spirit symbolized in the flame. The carrier of the torch is a descendant in spirit of the Alamo heroes; through them he becomes, according to this ritual, the legitimate heir to the Texas throne. He is delivered by the military, and he is welcomed by the citizenry as symbolized in the part of the ceremony in which the mayor of San Antonio offers him the key to the city.

In his new authority King Antonio LXIX ordered the end of the solemnity:

> King Antonio LXIX: This is my royal command to the people of San Antonio: Let your hands be joined together, let every heart be light, and to our visitors from far and near I say, "Welcome to our Fiesta and make it your own." . . . Commander, let the troops pass in review and be dismissed for merriment. Let the happy spirit of Fiesta rule our city. Viva Fiesta!

> (1991 Investiture of King Antonio)

The "troops" had served well in the eyes of their new king and deserved to be given leave to enjoy themselves.

But the merriment he ordered can come only after the annual Pilgrimage to the Alamo, occurring two days later, when civic groups within San Antonio bring flowers to honor the Alamo heroes. After all have paid homage to these dead, the festivities begin. Only after the pilgrimage will the new king make his triumphant entry into the heart of San Antonio on his river barge floating down the San Antonio River in the Texas Cavaliers' River Parade.

King Antonio LXIX's order was a promise and order of merriment to come in its proper *time* and *place*. This merriment is not to begin here in the light of evening sun and of remembrance fires burning. Such frivolity must not occur in front of the Alamo; this shrine is reserved for remembering the dead and birthing the new Texas society as embodied in the Texas Cavaliers.

Orders given by King Antonio throughout the investiture ceremony heighten the military aura of the site, group, and ceremony; the Alamo, as a shrine to Texas liberty, is religiously military, having received her baptism in the fire of battle. The merriment of Fiesta is foretold here, but does not take place here. Patriotism and homage are the proper behaviors in front of this shrine. The Alamo is the sacred site of transfiguration, as expressed on the south side of the cenotaph containing sculptor Pompeii Coppini's figure of sacrifice (Fig. 5.1).

And the Alamo is, according to the words of the Texas Cavaliers' ceremony outside the church, the site of their transformation from businessmen in San Antonio to defenders of Texas and the Alamo heritage. The Alamo, as the site of this transformation, is the womb to which these men return to be born into their new status during their secret ceremony inside, for it is at this time that the initiates are made Texas Cavaliers. Outside they are simply presented to the public; their metamorphosis has occurred inside the church. The privacy within the Alamo declares that these men have access to the womb's transformative power. Within the Alamo, they have knowledge of another sphere.

The outside world may not witness this transformation. What those outside the shrine see during this time is the Alamo glowing gold in the late afternoon/early evening sun. Not only is the site sacred; so is the time at which it occurs. According to the mythology, the heroes of the Alamo transform to spirit at this time of day in the flames of the funeral pyre. Released from the flesh, they go forth to enliven the hearts of all Texans. For the modern ceremony,

Fig. 5.1. South Side of the Alamo Cenotaph.

the Texas Cavaliers are inside the womb during this sacred time of day, being transformed; they will emerge to spread their own message to the outside world. But inside they use the sacredness of the place and of the time to make their communion with the Alamo heroes and with their deceased members, creating bonds of kinship between themselves and the dead.[5]

When they emerge, the Texas Cavaliers stress in their message to the outside world this communion they have had within the walls of the Alamo. In the prayer during the 1991 ceremony, former King Antonio Stanton Bell asked God to allow the metamorphosis for the Texas Cavaliers from businessmen to defenders. He connected the indomitable will he asked for the Texas Cavaliers to that allotted to the Alamo defenders in the Texas creation myth. He used the present tense when mentioning the heroes, emphasizing their continued presence in the shrine, their never-ending vigil over Texas: they are here now, as are the Texas Cavaliers, defenders of the shrine and Texas heritage.

Also forming a connection between the heroes of the past and the other Texas Cavaliers is the twenty-one-gun salute fired from a cannon behind the Long Barracks Museum. At the Alamo, cannon fire has great symbolic importance: Travis fired a cannon-shot response to Santa Anna's demand for surrender, a declaration that he would rather give up his life than give up the Alamo. But the twenty-one shots from the cannon during the new king's investiture constituted a signal of acceptance rather than denial. The Texas Cavaliers are on Travis's side of the mythological line, and cannon fire within the Alamo welcomes the new king.

The two military groups that approached the Alamo represent another link between the past and the present. The drill team from Fort Myer was the military present, and behind the present came the past, the Old Guard Fife and Drum Corps. The king-elect himself reflected the link between the two frames, arriving in a horse-drawn carriage depicting the past, yet wearing the modernized military uniform.

The figure of King Antonio mediates between the present and the past much as David Crockett mediates in the mythology between the barbarous past of the indigenous people and the present civilization of the Americans. But the king's figure is also connected to Travis in the direction from which he approaches the Alamo. He comes from out of the northeast corner, the same direction from which Travis came in his migration to Texas from South Carolina.

The history of the king's arrival adds another dimension to the symbolism here. The first King Antonio elected and invested by the Texas Cavaliers followed the pattern set by Fiesta kings in the first part of the twentieth century; he entered San Antonio by train, arriving from a secretly chosen station *east* of San Antonio. He was met at the Southern Pacific depot on Commerce Street by other Texas Cavaliers mounted on horses. Thus the new king came from out of the East, riding the iron horse of progress; the culture from which he came had built this technological wonder. The image is of an outsider, the stranger king, who rides into San Antonio to rule.

The early kings' procession from the depot to the Alamo echoed the procession that heralded the arrival of the first train in San Antonio. For that celebration Col. Thomas W. Pierce, the president of the railroad company responsible for building the Sunset Route, went to a town *east* of San Antonio, accompanied by the governor of Texas, Richard Hubbard, Lieutenant Governor Wells Thompson, and other state officials, railroad dignitaries, and army officers. When they arrived in San Antonio, they were met by the mayor of San Antonio, Henry French, who led the welcoming committee. All then proceeded to Alamo Plaza and gathered in front of the Menger Hotel, where socially prominent women greeted them from the balcony.[6] In front of this hotel, Governor Hubbard addressed the crowd and suggested that the railroad would not only tie East Texas to West Texas but would allow the businessmen of East Texas to meet (and marry) the "rosy-cheeked maidens" of San Antonio (*San Antonio Express*, February 20, 1877, as cited in Everett 1961:49–50).[7]

The railroad, in this history of the king's arrival, signals the beginning of San Antonio's exchange relationship with the cultured East, which sends money and men to San Antonio in exchange for natural resources, women, and raw products. The businessman, purveyor of progress, comes from the East to bring a new society and new blood to "the old, dry bones of the Alamo City" (*San Antonio Express* 1877, as cited in Everett 1961:48).

King Antonio, a prominent businessman in San Antonio then as today, embodies this progress. Similarly, symbolic of this progress, Travis comes from out of the East, with the law book in his hand, to bring a new order to Texas. As stranger from the East, Travis is a classic western hero.[8] The new King Antonio effects this distance of stranger by isolating himself from the other Texas Cavaliers during the day of his investiture. He does not attend the initiation of the new Texas Cavaliers. As one former King Antonio explained, the first time the Texas Cavaliers see him that day is when he approaches in his carriage to be invested as their new king.

Furthermore, Travis is tied to the northeastern direction not only by the origins of industry and government but also because the north wall of the Alamo is Travis's area to defend during the 1836 battle, and it is at this north wall that Travis dies. Thus the new leader of the Texas Cavaliers comes from the direction where the famous Alamo leader has lived and died.

King Antonio's transformation is to the role of leader and king of the renewed spirit of progress, annually celebrated at Fiesta. He follows in the footsteps of Travis, and he declares in his announcement of the names of the new Texas Cavalier members that these young men will also follow the lead of the heroic Alamo dead; he claims that they are the "worthy" ones of San Antonio who will carry forward the ideals of the Texas Cavaliers, ideals which, according to the Texas Cavaliers, are aligned with those of the Alamo defenders.

The only group other than the Texas Cavaliers allowed to socially reproduce inside the Alamo church is the Order of the Alamo. This group is less visible than the Texas Cavaliers during public functions; one reason for the lesser visibility is that some of the men who are members of the Order of the Alamo are also Texas Cavaliers and appear publicly with that group. Furthermore, the Order of the Alamo's main public ceremony features the city's wealthy debutantes as celebrated royalty, thus focusing on women rather than men.

Although the queen's selection and coronation is often cited as the Order of the Alamo's primary function, the declared purpose of the Order of the Alamo as stated in its bylaws holds no mention of the queen:

[This organization] is formed for the purpose of educating its members and the public generally in the history of the Independence of Texas and to perpetuate the memory of the battle of San Jacinto by having an annual ceremony to be held in the City of San Antonio, Bexar County, Texas.

(Order of the Alamo 1949:11)

The self-produced history of the organization states that the Order of the Alamo "accepted the responsibility for the Coronation and entertainment of the Queen and Princesses [sic]" as their means of "assisting San Antonio to preserve the memory of the patriotism, courage, and fortitude of those immortals responsible for the establishment of the grand empire of Texas" (Order of the Alamo 1975:no pagination). In his history of Fiesta, however, Maguire says that John

Carrington founded the organization because he felt that the selection of a queen to reign over the Battle of Flowers Parade was "too important to leave to chance or a whim." Maguire claims that Carrington wanted the Order of the Alamo to have as its only responsibility the choosing, coronation, and care of the queen (Maguire 1990:31).

From all appearances, the selection of the queen is indeed the primary function of the Order of the Alamo. Considering the social prestige associated with the position throughout this century, the queenship is the highest social honor the Order of the Alamo can award a family. What the Order of the Alamo creates inside the shrine when members select the queen and her court is the hierarchy of the most valuable wombs for social lines in San Antonio, born of those same lines.

The women's training to accept this role of continuing social connections begins at a very early age, as exemplified in the selection of four-year-old Caroline Basse to serve as a page to the princess in the 1989 coronation. The *North San Antonio Times* explores her background:

> The golden-haired daughter of Penne and Tres Basse is a symbol of generational friendship. Caroline's grandmother, Anne Wright Basse, was the queen a half century ago of the Order of the Alamo's Court of Music. A duchess in that 1939 coronation was Emily Bryant Browning. Emily's granddaughter, Emily Bryant Wilson, is this year's princess. Caroline will attend Princess Emily as royal page.
>
> . . . The beautiful monarch Anne Wright was escorted by Bruce Martindale. She is now married to Ed Basse, who was prime minister to Susan Gresham Davidge in 1947. Anne's royal pages were Benny Hammond and Joan Steves Devine. Joan is now the mother of the 1979 queen, Carroll Devine Nelson.
>
> . . . Anne has two sons, Gordon Leland and "Tres" Basse.
>
> In 1968 Anne and her princess, Evelyn White, watched their mutual niece, Tuleta Chittim White, ascend to the Order of the Alamo's throne. Her royal highness Evelyn was attended by pages, Merton Minter and Lucille Winerich Pipes. Following the Fiesta, Evelyn married her prince, Fred Thomson. Their daughter, Elizabeth Thomson Runion, was a page. After she was widowed, Princess Evelyn married 1936 Order president Harry Aflleck; his daughter, Ethel, was the 1971 Queen.
>
> On Fridays at the San Antonio Country Club Queen Anne and Duchesses Emily Bryant Browning, Kay Pardue Newton, Mary

Elizabeth Harper York, and Margaret Barclay Goldbury regularly convene for luncheon.

(Jacobs 1989:3; reprinted by permission of the Times Newspapers of San Antonio)

This is a typical lineage for a participant in the coronation. Annually the *North San Antonio Times* reports in its Fiesta supplement the lineages of certain participants in the coronation. As evident in the names Queen Anne and Princess Evelyn, the distinctions received at coronation last a lifetime.

The Order of the Alamo relishes this sense of lineage in the coronation. In its history, members imagine how a young woman must feel growing up within this social milieu:

Many a Duchess, Princess or Queen recalls an earlier day in Court when she toddled along as a page or entertainer. As she watched with amazement the dazzling spectacle before her, she dreamed, never realizing that it could come true, a day in which she might be proclaimed and honored in such a way.

(Order of the Alamo 1976:no pagination)

Such desire for continuity gives an inner-circle aura to the Order of the Alamo and their selection of the queen inside the Alamo. As one San Antonio reporter explains, "[F]or *Old* San Antonians, being in the Coronation is the ultimate social honor.... [Y]ou can't buy your way into the Coronation; you're born into it" (Pisano 1978:42). In a less-than-reverent tone, this reporter notes the maternal cast to the society surrounding these women:

[A] girl can be selected queen on the strength of her mother's social credentials and despite the fact that her father is an outsider. Daddies of the queen are automatically asked to become members of the Order. And the men who happen to marry duchesses are often welcomed into the group, even if they are nobodies. Marriage to royalty is an entree into the social set. The Coronation may be fantasy on a grand scale, but the doors it opens are very real.

(Pisano 1978:44)

For those women who wish to become Queen of the Order of the Alamo, this reporter offers the following checklist:

Be born into a very anglo, very old, Old San Antonio family. It helps if Momma was once a duchess or princess . . . better yet, a queen. (Note: When they carry you home from the maternity ward, look around. If it doesn't look like Terrell Hills, Olmos Park or Alamo Heights, your parents are probably nobodies. Go to Plan Two. Grow up, marry an eligible Old San Antonio bachelor and give this list to your daughter.)

When you're four or five, appear as a page for one of your relatives in Coronation. . . .

Take ballet at Amory Oliver's studio. . . .

Attend Alamo Heights High School (St. Mary's Hall is getting too nouveau). . . . Later go to UT or Princeton or some fashionable college in the Old South. Whatever you do, don't fall in love and settle down with some schlep back east. Newark doesn't have a Coronation.

Mingle with your social set. Play tennis at the club. Go to hunting parties at old family ranches. . . . Get Momma to call Alice Bonnett at the *North San Antonio Times* every day with news of your doin's. . . . Debut with the German Club. Get Daddy to spring for a lavish deb party at the San Antonio Country Club or the Argyle. . . .

Once you're named a duchess, get Daddy to take out a second mortgage on the house so you can have a spectacular gown. . . . Select the most up-and-coming bachelor member of the Order as your Duke (you may wind up marrying him). . . .

The next year, have Daddy button-hole all his hunting buddies in the Order and tell them what a swell queen you'd make. Get your aunts and cousins from past Coronations to write letters on your behalf. . . . *Voila*, you've made it. Reign majestically over the court. Wave to your subjects from a Battle of Flowers Parade float. Run up a big room service bill at your suite in the Menger.

(Pisano 1978:45)

Although the list is offered tongue-in-check, it points out some specific norms for those who wish to be part of the self-perpetuating social set of the Order of the Alamo (which intersects with the German Club and the Texas Cavaliers). The royal court personages come almost exclusively from sections on the north side of San Antonio that are independent municipalities, the area covered socially by the *North San Antonio Times*. A young woman wishing to be queen goes away for college, ideally to an Ivy League school, and then returns to San Antonio to be courted (in multiple senses of the word). As is King Antonio, she is someone with inside knowledge and breeding coming back in from the outside to reign. After her coronation, the queen moves into a suite in a downtown hotel, almost always the Menger Hotel on Alamo Plaza as it is usually the site of the Queen's Ball. She is thus close by the sacred shrine, the place of her persona's inception.

The ballots through which the Queen of the Order of the Alamo is determined are given to the president of the Order of the Alamo within the walls of the Alamo church in a private meeting. This meeting within the Alamo church is one of the two annual meetings held by the Order of the Alamo. (In the other meeting it elects its board of directors for the year; this meeting is held in the San Antonio Country Club.) Anthropologist Michaele Haynes, who has been interviewing people associated with the coronation of the Order of the Alamo court, was told that once inside the Alamo church, the members turn in their sealed ballots on which each member has written his first, second, and third choice for queen. Members must present their ballots in person (Haynes 1991).

The current selection of princess is a fairly simple matter; she is the first runner-up in the balloting for the queen. But in the past, the woman selected as queen chose her princess. The bylaws from the Order of the Alamo 1948–1949 annual report describe this selection: "The Princess, who is the Maid of Honor to the Queen, shall be selected by the Queen, but must be an unmarried lady who has been a resident of Bexar County, Texas for at least three years next preceding her selection" (Order of the Alamo 1949:23). The wording by the Order of the Alamo underscores the coronation's intended marriage-alliance orientation. The princess is the "maid of honor" chosen by the queen as a bride chooses the same. When she chooses who will serve as her escort (called duke if she is a duchess, prince if she is princess, and prime minister if she is queen), she selects from the bachelors in the Order of the Alamo. As Marina Pisano noted, the young woman ought to choose, according to the social rules, the most socially valuable member of the Order she can obtain as an escort, for she should consider him as a possible future husband.

The balloting that takes place inside the Alamo represents the union of all the socially prominent families' connections in San Antonio; the men pool their ballots, culminating in the birth of a queen and a princess from generations of the women's families who have proved socially worthy to reign in San Antonio society. The young women of these families assume the duty of continuing these social lines and of representing their family in the coronation.

On the night of coronation, these women, as gracefully as possible, pull across the Municipal Auditorium stage the heavy, ornate trains to their gowns, the symbol of their mother's social standing and their father's wealth. (The cost of these coronation gowns begins at around fifteen thousand dollars for a duchess's gown. The fathers of the queen and the princess must expect to spend at least twenty-five thousand dollars on their daughters' gowns.) Coronation is their duty as young women in the "old families" of San Antonio; it is their *work*.[9]

After the queen is crowned, she accompanies King Antonio on his visitations around San Antonio. (Prior to the coronation ceremony during Fiesta week, the queen from the previous year accompanies King Antonio.) Fiesta historian Jack Maguire professes not to understand why the king and queen are invested in different ceremonies "although both reign over the same loyal subjects" (Maguire 1990: 27). Maguire apparently has not considered the importance of age sets within Fiesta roles and within the mythology.

The usual difference in age sets between the king and the queen creates a father/daughter image. They travel together but are never considered a couple. This is the same age difference as that between William B. Travis and the infant Angelina Dickinson; Travis gives Angelina his engagement ring, but there is no romantic attachment intended. He is the ultimate hero, sacrificing his life so that Texas society may grow via Angelina, who is, according to the mythology, the most valuable womb inside the Alamo during the battle.

Angelina's primary value lies in eventually being able to reproduce; Travis's main value lies in his productivity as a military commander. The roles are similar for King Antonio and the Queen of the Order of the Alamo. King Antonio is an experienced, productive businessman in San Antonio society, and as such is usually older than the unmarried citizens of San Antonio; his main value lies in his *productivity*. The value of the Queen of the Order of the Alamo, however, lies in her *reproductive* potential, especially for reproducing descendants of San Antonio's "old families." As Pisano noted above, the mother's social background is more important when a young woman is considered for the coronation than is her father's social standing. The father must be able to provide the wealth for the making of the coronation gown; the mother provides the status within the community.

The following is a chart of age sets and roles of Fiesta participants involved in the coronation of the Queen of the Order of the Alamo and the investiture of King Antonio:

| Age Set | Male | Female |
|---|---|---|
| Children in Order of the Alamo Coronation | Page | Page |
| Young Adults (unmarried) in Order of the Alamo Coronation | Escorts | Members of the Court |
| Young Adults (unmarried) in Investiture of King Antonio | New Heroes | |
| Older Adults in Order of the Alamo Coronation | President<br><br>Lord High Chamberlain | Mistress of the Robes |
| Older Adults in Investiture of King Antonio | King | |

The Lord High Chamberlain serves as announcer for the members of the court, and the president of the Order of the Alamo assumes a role similar to the archbishop of Canterbury and crowns the queen.

The Mistress of the Robes is the only visible role for an older woman in the Fiesta investiture and coronation ceremonies. The bylaws of the Order of the Alamo describe her appointment and rule thus:

> The President shall on or before the election of the Queen, appoint . . . a married lady, who resides in Bexar County, Texas, and is approximately thirty-five years of age, Mistress of the Royal Robes, preference being given in such selection to the wives, mothers, or sisters of members of the Order. She shall be advised who has been elected Queen and who have been selected as other members of the Court. She shall assist in the selection of colors and costumes for the Court, and in such matters shall be the official representative of the Queen and Princess.
>
> (Order of the Alamo 1949:27–28)

The Mistress of the Robes is matronly, the experienced older woman who guides the young women through this rite of passage, keeping secret the identity of the queen and princess prior to coronation. As representative for these young women, she serves as mouthpiece for their wishes, protecting them from the outside world.

Within the Texas mythology, Susanna Dickinson plays such a role for her child, Angelina. She protects her from the desires of Santa Anna, refusing his offer to adopt the infant. She speaks for the child who cannot speak for herself. By Susanna's design, Angelina's reproductive years will not be spent in the company of the Mexican citizens. Susanna will direct Angelina's care and protect this young Texan womb from the victors of the Alamo battle.

The Alamo as stone womb of Texas society also has matronly custodians voicing her wishes and protecting her from violators: the Daughters of the Republic of Texas. All who would enter the Alamo for their own purposes must first win the favor of these women. But only two groups have won their favor: the Order of the Alamo and the Texas Cavaliers. These matrons carefully choose who may enter the Alamo unchaperoned. The DRT members absent themselves from their charge, the Alamo, when these two men's groups enter the stone womb.

# Chapter 6. Matronly Daughters

To be the Alamo's matron one must be a Daughter. These guardians, the Daughters of the Republic of Texas, are born to their role; in their eyes, it is their rightful place, inherited from patriotic ancestors. They take on the feminine role of preserving and honoring the memory of the men who, according to the mythology, bought Texas with their toil and their blood. The Alamo is the original birth site within this mythology, and the Daughters, as the state-appointed custodians, watch over the "cradle."

The DRT organization began in 1891 as the Daughters of the Lone Star Republic, but within a year of its founding, the members voted to change the organization's name to the Daughters of the Republic of Texas. Any woman wishing to be a Daughter must be at least eighteen years old and be able to trace ancestors to the early Anglo colonists of the 1820s or prove that her ancestors in Texas "aided in establishing the independence of Texas, or served the Republic of Texas in maintaining its independence" prior to its annexation to the United States in 1846 (DRT 1892:7).

The organization's constitution, printed in 1892, records its three objectives: (1) to foster the remembrance of the men and women who founded Texas; (2) to encourage historical research, especially from 1835 on; and (3) to promote the celebration of March 2 (anniversary of the signing of the Texas Declaration of Independence) and April 21 (anniversary of the San Jacinto battle), and to secure and preserve historic sites (DRT 1892:3–4).

Although not stated among the objectives, the DRT organization has, from its early years, sought a role in educating the public, especially children, about the post-1835 history of Texas. This education was initially part of the goal of having the state celebrate two dates in the Texas Revolution cited above. (The anniversary of the Alamo battle was not, as of 1892, considered a primary date.) In 1896, the DRT executive committee sent circulars to the schools throughout Texas asking that the schools hold ceremonies on these two dates. The *Texas School Journal* responded by requesting that the DRT prepare a program for the San Jacinto Day celebration. The DRT obliged this request that year with a program written by the chairman of the executive committee and the historian for the group, Adele B. Looscan.

In a program distributed for the 1901 celebration of San Jacinto Day, the DRT decided not only to remind the students of the importance of April 21, but also to promote the importance of the DRT via a segment of the program conducted as a dialogue between the teacher and her or his pupils:

[Q] Have the cities and towns in which these historic events took
place been careful to preserve and mark these memorable spots
as they should be?
[A] In many instances, no.
[Q] What society was organized for this purpose?
[A] The Daughters of the Republic of Texas.
[Q] How do they expect to do this?
[A] By arousing public sentiment to the importance of locating
and preserving these historic places and traditions.
[Q] Why do they wish to do this?
[A] From motives of State love and pride; and because one of the
strongest incentives to a nation's patriotism and loyalty is the
perpetuation of the names and deeds and places made famous
and sacred by these acts of bravery and daring.

(DRT 1901 : no pagination)

The DRT, according to this dialogue, has as its primary function the preservation of the past, a duty the members perform out of "love and pride," emotions which transcend the male world of war and economics and define the world of women and children.

At the DRT's second annual meeting, the woman's role (and particularly the role of these women) in educating Texas' children appears in the address by the DRT president, Mrs. Anson Jones:

[Texas'] future is in the hands of her sons. Daily they go forth
to achieve great things, and we must not blame them if, strong
in their own strength, dazzled by the splendor of the present,
they have somewhat forgotten the heroic deeds and sacrifices
of the past. But it is not so with woman. Her work lies at home.
Surrounded by the history of the family life, it is her duty to keep

alive the sacred fire of tradition. The struggle for to-day and ambition for to-morrow do not crowd out of her heart grateful memories of yesterday. At the fireside, and for the most part in the school room, the children are hers. Her influence can bend their young minds whither she will. And so it seems to me, Daughters of the Republic of Texas, our duty lies plain before us. Let us leave the future of Texas to our brothers, and claim as our province the guarding of her holy past. . . . Let us love to study Texas history and teach it to her children.

(DRT 1893:2–3)

According to this ideology, men hold in their hands the future, women the past. The domain of men is the public business world, and their duty is to create wealth; the domain of women is the privacy of "home," and their duty is to preserve the past through educating the children, "bend[ing] their young minds."

The "homes" where Texas history can be taught are not only the individual residences and classrooms, but the historic sites as well. From its early years, the DRT organization has made acquiring the custodianship of these sites one of its objectives. At its 1898 annual meeting the DRT announced that the organization had received custodianship of the first capitol building of the Texas Republic; in 1905 the DRT obtained custody of the state-owned portion of the Alamo compound; in 1926 it obtained use of the Old Land Office in Austin as its headquarters and DRT museum; and in 1937 the organization located and purchased the building, now known by the DRT as "The Cradle" of their organization (being the building in which the DRT's founding members, Betty Ballinger and Hally Bryan, "conceived" the organization).

Protecting heritage is the declared interest of the DRT as well as of another group of Daughters which also formed in 1891: the Daughters of the American Revolution. Journalists then and now have occasionally confused the two organizations. For example, a 1906 headline in the San Antonio Gazette read: "De Zavala Chapter D.A.R. Wins Alamo"; and a 1987 headline in the San Antonio Express-News read: "DAR Against Alamo Buses Ban."

The DAR's group name focuses on the revolution (the significance of the "R") and thus on the action and sacrifice associated with fighting. Although the "R" in DRT focuses on the independence of Texas as a republic, there is a common confusion with revolution and the sacrifice necessary to birth a nation, a confusion which the DRT as a body does not seem to mind. Shortly after its inception, the DRT described its membership as "the widows, wives, daughters and female descendents of the early pioneers of Texas, who made the matchless history of our State, and sacrificed life and property for the benefit of humanity" (Looscan 1904:81). The role of all these "early pioneers" becomes remarkably similar to that described for the Alamo defenders (i.e., sacrificing life and property). At the time this description was written, the DRT was pushing to obtain custody of the Alamo church and the Long Barracks; the members appear as the rightful heirs to this sacred site as the female descendants of sacrificial men.

The desire for a heroic sacrificial image makes Susanna Dickinson and her infant daughter invaluable components within the creation mythology; Susanna and Angelina become the original widow and daughter within the church walls. The DRT's ongoing presence at the site reinforces this image, and many of the visitors to the Alamo misunderstand the members' "daughter" descendancy as being from the Alamo defenders.

The desire for such ancestry reflects the late-nineteenth-century interest in historical pageantry mentioned previously. The DRT's founding is part of the practice in the United States of connecting ancestors to the region's "unique" past. The organization formed in the same year as the first Battle of Flowers Parade and the subsequent forming of the Battle of Flowers Association (BOFA). Both groups focus on local history as their *raison d'être*, with the Alamo as center of the past and San Antonio's uniqueness. But the two groups do not have the same people within them.[1] The DRT's explicit descendancy requirement is one of the main dividing lines between the two groups. DRT members can be BOFA members, but unless a BOFA member can trace roots back to pre-1846 Texas, she cannot be part of the DRT.

According to the Texas creation mythology, the primary site that creates a uniqueness for Texas is the Alamo, so it became an important site for the DRT to claim. Although the purpose statement of the DRT does not specifically mention the care of the Alamo as one of its primary objectives, a historian of the DRT, Jack Butterfield, declares that "the chief concern of the Daughters is, naturally, the Alamo" (Butterfield 1960:4).

Not all members of the DRT organization are immediately involved in the administration of the Alamo. There are several chapters of the DRT, and although the entire organization was given custodianship of the Alamo by the State of Texas in 1905, it is primarily the Alamo Chapter, located in San Antonio, that is directly involved with the site's care.

The members of the Alamo Chapter accept their role as custodians of this site as a mother would care for an adopted child, giving
their time free of charge. They feel that they carry out their role as
custodians exceedingly well, and because of their efforts the Alamo
should honor not only the sacrifice of its famous male heroes, but
the fortitude of its female protectors as well. The Daughters declare
that the Alamo is more than a shrine to the Alamo defenders; it is
also "a monument to the courage, zeal and patriotism of the Daughters of the Republic of Texas as its designated custodians" (DRT
1990a: 3).

If the Alamo defenders were the protectors of Texas' liberty, saving her life in their sacrifice to buy time, the Daughters claim they
have rescued the Alamo, the cradle of Texas liberty. In the DRT's
history of the shrine, the creation mythology stretches out to en-
compass not only the male trinity of Bowie, Crockett, and Travis,
but also a figure within the DRT: Miss Clara Driscoll. A Daughter
and heir to this mythological womb, Driscoll purportedly sacrifices
property at the turn of the century to "save the Alamo" from falling
into the hands of commercialism:

> That old Alamo Mission with its building and grounds, the sa-
> cred spot made dear to the heart of every Texan by reason of its
> baptism in the blood of heroes, is now placed within reach of our
> people only by the patriotic devotion of Miss Clara Driscoll, one
> of the Daughters of the Republic, who, by her generous act in ad-
> vancing over seventeen thousand dollars from her own private
> funds, in order to preserve it from the relentless grasp of com-
> mercial greed, has made it possible that the whole of the Alamo
> may yet become the property of the people of Texas, and be for-
> ever preserved as a shrine before which future generations should
> stand in reverent deference.
>
> (Looscan 1904: 81–82)[2]

In the DRT scenario, this unmarried Daughter offers her private
property for the good of the public. She becomes the "guardian angel," caring for the defenseless Alamo in the face of a progress that
would destroy the serenity of the "home."

Clara Driscoll has been the "guardian angel" of the site since her
rise to renown in Texas; a 1936 newspaper article declared her as
such, and *Texas Monthly* echoed the sentiment by titling a January
1986 article about her "The Guardian." Both 1936 and 1986 are significant years (the centennial and the sesquicentennial of Texas' in-

dependence from Mexico), and Clara Driscoll's appearance in print as Alamo guardian reveals the mythic status she has within the Alamo's past.

The 1904 description of Driscoll is part of the previously referenced plea to the Legislature to reimburse the down payment on the Long Barracks. In this plea, the Alamo church, the site popularly known as the Alamo, is not distinguished from the property "rescued" by Driscoll. A 1990 description, offered by the DRT, of Driscoll's purchase makes the distinction a little more clear but still leaves some ambiguity:

> Interest in preserving the Alamo and cherishing it as a historic spot began in 1903. At this time, the large area to the north of the Alamo Shrine was owned and occupied by the Hugo-Schmeltzer Company, wholesale merchants. In that same year, the company announced that it was going out of business and offered its property for sale. A syndicate was formed for the purpose of buying the property and erecting a hotel. A young woman named Clara Driscoll, who was a member of the Daughters of the Republic of Texas, heard about this plan through Adina De Zavala and began to take steps to prevent the eventual desecration of the Alamo and its grounds.
>
> (DRT 1990a: 3)

The DRT notes that the property Driscoll salvaged was "the large area to the north of the Alamo Shrine," and yet DRT members speak of the "eventual desecration of the Alamo," implying that the building popularly known as the Alamo would be involved in the commercial property.

Historian Jack Butterfield is similarly confusing in his description of the area endangered. He notes that the property for sale was not the shrine itself; but he then states, "When it appeared that the Daughters of the Republic of Texas had lost the struggle to save the Alamo, Miss Clara Driscoll . . . paid $500.00 for an option for one month" (Butterfield 1960: 7). Again the implication is that the property for sale somehow involved the famous church. This confusion is shared by some of the DRT members; one member told me that Clara Driscoll bought and saved the Alamo church, denying information I offered to the contrary.

A few historians have tried to dispel this part of the DRT's mythology. The director of the Texas Historical Commission (THC) Landmarks Office, Jim Steely, is one such historian. In a small publication of the THC he writes, "One of the most oft-repeated legends of the Alamo . . . is that Clara Driscoll 'saved the Alamo.' " Steely then offers an account of the transactions involved:

> Deed records of the transaction show that . . . she supplied the $25,000 down payment on property *adjacent* to the old mission church. . . . Indeed, the old mission church, which Texans associate most strongly with the events of 1836, had been owned by the state since its purchase in 1883 from the Roman Catholic Church. . . . What Clara Driscoll bought in 1904 was part of the mission's *convento.*
>
> (Steely 1990:5)

Steely declares at the end of his article that the people who actually "saved" the Alamo church were earlier Texans, such as Samuel Maverick, various Catholic bishops, and the U.S. Army.

Steely braves the wrath of the DRT in one sense by "correcting" one of their favorite stories (i.e., Clara Driscoll saved the church). But the *building* involved is only one of the issues at stake in the DRT's pride in Clara Driscoll. Neither Steely nor Butterfield touches this second sore point; neither one mentions within his account of Driscoll's purchase on Alamo Plaza the name of Adina De Zavala. The DRT's version mentions her, but that she is little more than a medium through which the message passes, much like a telephone line.

Herein lies the more controversial issue: *Who* within the DRT saved the Alamo—Driscoll or De Zavala? The savior role became a bone of contention in 1905 when Driscoll and De Zavala disagreed on who should dictate the care of the site, particularly in regards to the Long Barracks, once it had been "rescued" from commercial hands. The women entered into a tug-of-war for control of the site; a journalist of the time recognized the deeper meaning of the struggle:

> It is a war of women, a fight for fame and favors, a battle for honors socially and historically distinctive. . . . It all began when the executive committee of the Daughters of the Republic voted that in recognition of her personal interest in saving the Alamo for the States [*sic*] of Texas, Miss Driscoll should be honored by appointment as custodian of the building for one year. This is no mean honor, for all the thousands of visitors who go annually to beautiful San Antonio visit, first of all the interesting sights

there, the one great historical monument to the bravery and patriotism of Texas—the Alamo. As its custodian Miss Driscoll
would receive many attentions and be much honored.

("Fight for Queen of the Alamo": 1905)

In this battle, one Daughter will come out the victor, being granted
the honor of primary guardian within a group of custodians. The
fight, according to this journalist, is to be "Queen of the Alamo."
The dispute begun in 1905 has new social tones now. Although
most informants agree that the dispute between Adina De Zavala
and Clara Driscoll was not initially an ethnic one, it has become
ethnically oriented. De Zavala, primarily because of her surname
and ancestry, is the favorite of many Hispanics interested in this
purported rescue of the Alamo battleground. According to the pro–
De Zavala version, De Zavala heard about the possible sale of the
convento/Long Barracks building and worked to save it; Driscoll
simply supplied the money. But within the DRT's mythology surrounding the Alamo's rescue by Clara Driscoll, De Zavala becomes
a minor and disappearing heroine who is only *initially* useful.[3]
De Zavala's name and influence disappear in the DRT version after
the Alamo has been saved from commercial grasp. It is Driscoll who
heroically fights back the aggressive male business world from the
defenseless shrine and who helps the DRT win custody of the Alamo
after "a long, hard fight" (Butterfield 1960:8).
    In contrast, the pro–De Zavala version creates the image of Clara
Driscoll as the tyrant who cares more for the social recognition she
gains in "saving the Alamo" than she does for the site itself. In this
version, Driscoll is actually the destroyer of the sacred battlefield;
in her historical ignorance, she has the second story of the *convento*
razed so that the Alamo church stands taller and more prominently
than the *convento*. This version's true heroine is De Zavala, who
tries in vain to stop Driscoll's desecration of a hallowed building
"baptized in the blood of heroes."
    Despite all her hard work (according to De Zavala supporters),
De Zavala receives ruthless treatment from the wealthy Driscoll
and her followers; De Zavala and her faithful band are dragged
through court battle after court battle by the Driscollites. When
Driscoll wins her final victory in court, she has De Zavala and
the rest of her DRT chapter disenfranchised from the organization.
Then Driscoll takes to the limelight, reveling in her reign over the
Alamo. Driscoll ascends the throne as Queen of Fiesta for three
straight years, supposedly in recognition of her role as savior of the

Alamo. Meanwhile, De Zavala devotes herself to the serious but less glorified work of historical conservation. At De Zavala's death, her funeral procession may only pass by her beloved Alamo out in the street, whereas Driscoll, upon her death, lies in state inside the church (Ables 1967). The distinction between inside and outside privileges becomes clear.

For *whatever* reason, there is a heavier historical emphasis on Driscoll than on De Zavala in DRT-controlled space. The two women's presence in the narratives at the Alamo site, particularly inside and outside the Long Barracks Museum, reveals this imbalance. At one end of this building is the Clara Driscoll Theater, a small room in which plays a videotaped narrative of the Alamo's past. Driscoll's portrait hangs on the wall behind the television monitor playing the videotape, and her piano stands against a side wall near the portrait. At the end of the tape appears the DRT's explanation that they have created this narrative "as a memorial to the 'Savior of the Alamo.' "

In the central section of the Long Barracks Museum is a display entitled "Saving the Alamo," which contains a narrative describing the DRT purchase of the Long Barracks building. Both the names of Adina De Zavala and Clara Driscoll appear in this narrative. But within this section Driscoll's photograph is enclosed in a glass case containing artifacts from her personal and public life (her Texas flag, her sash and pin as past state president of the DRT, and a pamphlet about her by Jack Butterfield); protected by enclosure, Driscoll's presence has value. In contrast, De Zavala's photograph is in the open, surrounded only by photographs of exterior walls.

Driscoll's primary recognition at this building, however, appears on its outside. Centered on the exterior wall within the courtyard is a display dedicating the site to Clara Driscoll. Under her likeness is a narrative of her contribution:

Despite many battles, the greatest threat to the survival of the Alamo occurred in the early 1900's. . . . Anxious businessmen wanted to tear down the barracks part of the Alamo and build a hotel on the site. Ironically, the main area of the 1836 Battle of the Alamo was about to be lost to "progress."[4] However, before the Alamo could fall this time, a high-spirited young woman, Clara Driscoll, rescued the Texas shrine.

· · ·

Clara Driscoll died July 17, 1945, in Corpus Christi. Her body lay in state in the Alamo and services were held in St. Mark's Episcopal Church. Miss Driscoll's body was buried in the Alamo Masonic Cemetery in the family mausoleum along with her father and brother, but her spirit lives within the Alamo.

Clara Driscoll thus appears (in her likenesses) in the Long Barracks, and according to the mythology, her spirit lives on within the Alamo, as do the spirits of the defenders.

But the Driscoll name and image did not always so dominate this site. In the early 1900s there was a plaque to the De Zavala Chapter of the DRT on what De Zavala called "the main building." In the heat of the Driscoll–De Zavala dispute, the plaque was plastered over.[5] In a collection of De Zavala's personal papers (on file in the Barker Library in Austin) are photographs of the covered plaque. According to De Zavala's notations on the backs of various photographs of this covered plaque, the plastering occurred during the 1907 Convention of the National and International Federation of Women's Clubs and was done by DRT members in authority at the Alamo church. De Zavala wrote that the reason the plaque was covered was to obscure the work done by the members of the De Zavala Chapter of the DRT.[6] The De Zavala name in this scenario denoted an entire faction within the DRT; it was not part of an *ethnic* struggle at the time but a personal one.

But this past erasure of a Hispanic name has become an ethnic issue. The treatment in print of the two women and the credit each desires continues to be a sore point, especially with some of the Hispanics. Steely's neglect of De Zavala's role riled Henry Guerra, a well-known Hispanic businessman in San Antonio and chairman of the Bexar County Historical Society. He wrote this response to Steely's article:

> I must question the omission of the name of Adina De Zavala. It was she who had organized the first chapter of the Daughters of the Republic of Texas and had begun the fight to preserve and restore the Alamo. And it was she who first called on Miss Driscoll, who had just returned from a European tour and was staying at the Menger Hotel. And it was she, by all accounts, who persuaded the young Miss Driscoll to provide the funding to protect the Alamo's Long Barracks from the developers.
>
> (Guerra 1990a)

Guerra is strong enough within San Antonio society not to fear reprisals from the DRT, and he continues to question the omission of

Hispanic figures and the lower status of Hispanics in Texas history. Jim Steely, in response to Guerra's protest, wrote an article a year later outlining De Zavala's role in Driscoll's purchase of the *convento* and De Zavala's attempts to stop Driscoll's demolition of the second story (Steely 1991 : 5).

In a reverse situation, a journalist who showered accolades on De Zavala found himself besieged by the DRT. In February 1961 Frank Tolbert wrote an article entitled "Lone Woman Defended Alamo in Battle of '05" in which he explained that De Zavala "fought off the hotel syndicate agents to arouse interest in preserving the historic mission" (Tolbert 1961a). This recognition of De Zavala instead of Driscoll as the lone woman defending the Alamo must have brought the wrath of the DRT down on Tolbert. When three months later he wrote a second article entitled "About Great Lady Who Owned Alamo," he prefaced the article with this explanation: "The Daughters of the Republic of Texas have asked me to rare [*sic*] back and recite a piece on one of this state's most memorable women, the late Clara Driscoll. . . . [T]he DRT hath spoken" (Tolbert 1961b). Tolbert then gratified the DRT's desire for public recognition of Driscoll's value.

The DRT's sensitivity to the issue pushes against De Zavala's image at the site as well. One woman working in the Alamo museum complex explained to me that new findings on the event suggest that Clara Driscoll had already conceived of saving the Alamo before she ever met with De Zavala. These "new findings" further diminish De Zavala in the rescue of the Alamo battlefield, leaving Driscoll as the lone defender in the 1905 battle. In modern eyes, the contest is between the Anglos and the Hispanics as to who will be the descendant of the Alamo's heritage; in this fight, as in the 1836 Alamo battle, the Hispanics become the disenfranchised kin.[7]

# Chapter 7. Adopted Daughter

In the past presented at the Alamo, the struggle continues for recognition of favorite characters and images. If one Daughter of Hispanic heritage—Adina De Zavala—is rejected, another daughter—the Alamo itself—is adopted. Separated from its "sister missions," the Alamo loses its former Fathers and Brothers, never again to be in the same "family."

The first separation from the Catholic clerical family came in 1793 with the secularization of the Mission San Antonio de Valero. In 1802 the compound came under the wing of San Carlos de Parras del Alamo and his Flying Company, and the site later hosted various other military corps. The Alamo's transformation to its ultimate status among a new people occurs, according to the Texas creation mythology, during the 1836 Alamo battle. Here she is baptized by blood and fire, and the Texans claim her as the fertile ground in which they will plant the seed of liberty. She is now sacred, having been hallowed by Travis's sword and the Texans' deaths within her.

The Alamo's separation from the other missions is a recurrent theme in San Antonio. When representations of the five missions do appear together, the Alamo is often set off from the others. One of the most recent and visible of such depictions is part of a large-scale renovation and development of downtown San Antonio. On the Houston Street bridge over the San Antonio River, four columns have been erected, each dedicated to one of the missions on the San Antonio Mission Trail (Fig. 7.1). Each column has an image, painted on ceramic tiles, of its designated mission, and the mileage down the river to the mission is indicated. The Alamo does not appear on a column; but towering over the Houston Street bridge on the facade of the Texas Theater, four replicas of the Alamo adorn the corners. An architect involved in the site choice for the mission columns acknowledged that the Texas Theater's facade influenced the choice of the Houston Street bridge, but only because of the terra cotta

Fig. 7.1. Representations of the Missions on the Houston Street Bridge.

colors within it, not the representation of the Alamo itself; the reunion of the five missions at the Houston Street bridge, according to this architect, was coincidental.

*Possibly* that union/distinction of the missions and their status is coincidental; but the 1991 placement of the mission facades at the Night in Old San Antonio Fiesta event reflects a planned separation. During the 1991 Fiesta San Antonio, plywood replicas of the missions' facades were created for the new NIOSA section "Mission Trail." On the outer wall of the section, the replicas of the four missions composing the Mission Trail were placed together, with the plywood pieces overlapping one another. The Alamo's replica was isolated from the others; it was placed opposite the outer wall and on the entrance to the next NIOSA section, the "French Quarter."

The separation of the Alamo from the other missions was emphasized in the inauguration of this new section. The NIOSA sponsor, the San Antonio Conservation Society, asked Rev. Balthazar Janacek, Director of the Spanish Missions, to perform the inauguration. Janacek spoke first of the need for unity within San Antonio, and then had the acolyte assisting him bring forward a bowl of water. He blessed the water, took the aspergillum, and flung water on the four mission facades on the outer wall, blessing each one individually. The Alamo facade he left dry and unblessed.

When asked about his neglect of the Alamo facade, Janacek replied, "I didn't see it . . . I thought it was just a sign." He then explained the difference between the Alamo and the other four missions: "The four missions are alive as centers of worship. . . . The Alamo is a museum" (Janacek 1991). As a museum, the Alamo is host to what is past, serving the deceased. The Alamo is dead to her former place within the Catholic church; she is no longer part of the same family as her "sister missions." In the eyes of Janacek, the Alamo church, as a museum, is dead and celebrates the dead.

This claim that the dead are the focus at the Alamo shrine does not clash with the DRT's understanding of the site's purpose. The Daughters accept the dead as their focus, but the dead honored at the Alamo are from a select group. Anyone attempting to honor *all* who died at the 1836 battle—including the Mexican dead—receives the scorn of the DRT. It appears that the DRT members wish, as much as possible, to keep Hispanic claims to the site to a minimum; the shrine must be separated from its sister missions, and it must serve to venerate Texans, not Mexicans.

In the eyes of some DRT members involved with the care of the Alamo, one of the most offensive ways that Hispanics can cling to their mother country is to try to honor the Mexican dead of the 1836

Alamo battle. However, such honor was requested by the executive director of the Texas Historical Commission, Curtis Tunnell. The DRT Alamo Chapter had asked Tunnell to speak at its 1990 March 6 memorial service inside the Alamo church, and in his speech he called for consideration of the Mexican soldiers in the 1836 battle:

> At the Alamo in March of 1836, there were those who . . . chose to be here because they believed that their cause was just. There were others who died here while serving their country as conscripts. Certainly there were good men and there were brave men who died on *both* sides of these walls during those days. . . . Today I hope we will set aside any lingering question or controversies, and while we are memorializing our greatest heroes, let us also honor and remember all the good men and the brave men who gave their lives in this great battle, a battle which has played such a difficult role in shaping this wonderful state of Texas that all of us enjoy today.
>
> (1990 DRT *Annual Memorial Service for the Heroes of the Alamo*)

Tunnell requires a new interpretation of the people involved in the 1836 battle. But this speech appears to have passed unheeded by the DRT members in attendance. Honoring of the Mexican soldiers is still not part of the history presented by the DRT at the Alamo; the ceremonies and the instruction offered there reinforce, instead, the story line of the Texas creation mythology, with only the "defenders" as the honored dead. To do otherwise would (in the eyes of at least one DRT member) simply be putting history through a civil rights filter.

The purportedly "unfiltered history" is what the Alamo Chapter offers at the site. The majority of the DRT-sponsored instruction of the public is done on an everyday basis at the Alamo compound with the church as the most sacred arena. The atmosphere inside the church is reverent: the Daughters ask that men remove their hats and that all visitors speak in hushed voice. Only the guides speak in elevated tone during their reciting of the site's history.

These recitations take place in the part of the church where the altar would have been, just above the juncture of the cross. At this spot in the building stands a model of the Alamo compound as it is supposed to have looked during the 1836 siege, minus figurines. The lack of figurines in this model contrasts with the use of figurines in the model within the Alamo gift shop. The shrine's image must be of eternal life (hero status) gained through supreme sacrifice. The

Alamo, in this ideology, is an empty tomb. There should be no dead bodies, even in figurines, in the past presented inside the Alamo church. (In the gift shop, however, the fighting and death imagery is a big boost to sales of rifles, miniature cannon, coonskin hats, and books about the battle, so bodies abound in the gift shop's model.)

Above the church's model of the battle site hang the "six flags over Texas": Spanish, French, Mexican, Republic of Texas, Confederate, and United States. Before the hourly recitation begins, the guide instructs visitors wishing to hear the talk to gather under the six flags. Here the guide uses the model during the talk to point out where particular events occurred. Having been told they are in a shrine and therefore should not applaud, the audience silently dissipates when the talk is over. The aura is similar to that of a sermon in which the faithful have been given the truth and are then sent to carry that knowledge with them to the outside world.

According to a DRT member, the history talk is the only "tour" conducted on a daily basis. Special tours are offered to visiting dignitaries, such as Queen Elizabeth II, and to school-aged children on field trips. Tours given for tourists and field trips are guided by people the DRT Alamo Chapter has trained in the site's significance.

The tours conducted for schoolchildren are more openly didactic than those offered the general public. On one tour given in 1990 for a group of fourth graders from a Texas elementary school, the guide offered a general history of the site as the group stood around the model of the Alamo compound, but he would stop occasionally and ask the children if they knew the answers to certain questions, such as, "Who was the one man who did not cross Travis's line?" and "How many soldiers did Santa Anna have at the Alamo?" He would then supply the answers or confirm the children's responses.

Each part of the museum on such tours is carefully interpreted by the guide with its significance made clear. On this tour for fourth graders, the guide took the children around the building, pointing out paintings, objects in glass cases, and the importance of each room within the church. When he came to the room to the immediate right (when facing the main doors from the inside) of the Alamo's entrance, he declared that this room, which had served as a confessional during the mission period, was possibly where Bowie had died. This room thus received great importance at the Alamo: here the sins of a past life had been forgiven, both via confessions and via Bowie's death in defense of Texas.

Immediately after this point in this particular tour, one of the fourth-grade teachers asked where Susanna Dickinson had been during the battle, and the guide, pointing to the room immediately to the left of the entrance, answered, "She's right there," giving a presence to Susanna in the room. When later examining the room, the guide explained that this room was where women and children stayed during the battle, and he said that the room was probably where Travis gave Angelina his ring. Thus, facing one another in the church, according to the guide's information, are rooms containing absolution and death in one and promise of new life in the other.

This oppositional placement of Bowie's death and the presence of Susanna and Angelina Dickinson in the Alamo church appears to be the accepted story line inside the shrine. Another guide offered the same information in 1993 when asked where Bowie died and where Susanna and Angelina stayed during the battle. But this placement of Bowie's death in the Alamo church is surprising, since most accounts of Bowie's death have him dying in the second story of the Long Barracks (part of which was serving as a hospital during the siege) or in the barracks to the right of the Alamo gate, where Bowie had his headquarters. Even Walter Lord's account *A Time to Stand*, the version of the Alamo battle most revered by many Texas historians and by the DRT, has Bowie die in the barracks by the gate (cf. Lord 1961:165).

However, the DRT organization (which trains the tour guides) is in control of history in the shrine, and they choose to place Bowie's death inside the church walls. The DRT's educational packet, which is offered to schoolteachers, declares that Bowie died inside the church: "Gradually the Texans fell, the last eleven killed inside the Church. Jim Bowie was one of these men. He died fighting from his cot, still bedridden from sickness" (Lindsay 1990:7). The author of this section cites as one of her two sources Lord's *Time to Stand* (the other is *The Alamo Mission: San Antonio de Valero, 1718–1793* by Father Marion Alphonse Habig). Despite Lord's placement of Bowie's death in the barracks, the DRT writer decides to place his death inside the church, adding a battle significance to the Catholic confessional.

The DRT may be hesitant to suggest that Bowie died in the hospital part of the Long Barracks because Clara Driscoll had that part of the building destroyed after her court victory over Adina De Zavala. It is also important to the DRT that Bowie's death not occur where his quarters once stood; the building, if it were still standing, would be on city property and thus out of the hands of the DRT. The DRT's hold on Alamo Plaza is limited; the state-owned property under DRT custody is less than half of the historic battle site. The Daughters must fit as much significance as possible into the ground they control. Thus they work, through the misinformation given visitors and schoolteachers, to keep Bowie's image inside the Alamo church walls.

The individual rooms in the church are closed to visitors via rope barriers, but the visitors may peer into the rooms. In the front part of the church (where the congregation would have gathered) are glass cases containing artifacts, most of which pertain to David Crockett, William B. Travis, James Bowie, and James Bonham. Each of these men is present in the Alamo via their personal effects encased in glass. They have value and are protected not only by the cases, but by an armed Alamo Ranger stationed inside the church.[1] As one Alamo Ranger explained, the value of these items is one of the reasons the Alamo Rangers must carry guns. The heroes as present in these artifacts must be protected.

Less-valued artifacts of other early Texans and artifacts of "progress," such as barbed wire, appear in cases inside the Alamo gift shop/museum. The primary Texas figure honored in this other building is Sam Houston, the victor of San Jacinto who became president of the Texas Republic. On the wall over the entrance to the building is a plaster model of Houston's gravestone in Huntsville, Texas. Glass cases contain items he carved, an invitation to his presidential inaugural ball, personal possessions of his children, and pictures of him, his wife, and his house in Huntsville, among other things. Other cases within the center of this building contain items depicting survival in this wilderness and its ultimate taming, such as branding irons. These cases stand primarily in the center of the building; to either side are cases full of souvenirs available for purchase: Alamo replicas, fake coonskin hats, miniature cannon, books about the Alamo, postcards, jewelry, Alamo cookie cutters, and many other items.[2]

The placement of artifacts and souvenirs echoes the center/periphery relationship of the Alamo and tourist businesses surrounding it; the Alamo is the "really real" center, and reproductions (e.g., the wax museum and the IMAX theater) surround it. The cases in the middle of the gift shop/museum contain "the real thing," artifacts of the past which are priceless and untouchable. The cases to either side contain the priced reminiscences for purchase and handling by the tourists.

Other than the church, the gift shop/museum, the Long Barracks, and the DRT Library, the only other buildings on the site are the administrative building on the east end of the property (with public rest rooms connected to it) and Alamo Hall, which is on the south side. Of these two areas, Alamo Hall is the more important to the DRT, for it contains the Alamo Committee Room, where decisions about the Alamo's care are made. The DRT Alamo Chapter holds its March 2 celebration of the signing of the Texas Declaration of Independence outside Alamo Hall.

The most likely places to find Daughters on the state-owned property are the gift shop and Alamo Hall. They almost certainly will not be out in front of the Alamo church; they remain inside the walls enclosing the state-owned portion of the Alamo compound, the feminine arena protected by the Alamo Rangers, both within and without.[3] In this enclosure, the women care for the "cradle" and cultivate the gardens planted on ground mythologically blessed by the heroes' blood.[4]

The current gardens on the site continue the order-from-chaos theme of the Texas creation mythology. Two of the gardens on the Alamo grounds are particularly representative of this theme in which the separation of types (i.e., cultivated versus wild) is apparent. Each of these gardens occupies a lawn-size expanse and reflects the stereotypical flora of either the untamed Southwest or the cultivated Old South.

The garden associated with the Southwest contains various cacti and other desert plants. These plants appear to be growing without order or formation, and at their base is white rock, adding to the dry, uncultivated quality of this garden. Across from this apparently arid section, separated from it by a cement walk, is the other garden, a lawn of thick, green grass associated with homes of the Old South. In the center of this lawn stands an oak tree (*Quercus virginia*) with a plaque declaring that the tree is dedicated to the memory of the heroes of the Alamo. In each of the two near corners of the lawn is a well-trimmed rose garden, surrounded by the green grass.

The soft green of this lawn is juxtaposed to the dry, desert quality of the cactus garden, the wild, native life devoid of the order that cultivated life offers. The lush lawn not only represents culture (and therefore productivity); it also represents reproductivity. The oak tree is masculine both in its honoring of the heroes of the Alamo and in its production of seed (acorns). In type, Virginian, it is the established order of such society founders as John Carrington with his First Families of Virginia credentials; the Virginian is the epitome of culture, both colonial and southern. On either side of this cultural archetype grows femininity expressed in the supreme cultured flower: the rose.

The rose, as a symbol, is closely associated with the Alamo itself, as is exemplified on the cover of the official daily program of Fiesta 1912 (Fig. 7.2). The Alamo blooms as the center of "the rose we all love"; the shrine contains the rose's cultured fertility. The rose's

Fig. 7.2. Program Cover for the 1912 Fiesta San Jacinto.

(and the Alamo's) femininity, in conjunction with the male Virginia seed, reflect the Culture and productivity of the land in Anglo Texan hands.

The rose as Alamo symbol was expressed during Queen Elizabeth's 1991 visit to the Alamo. When she emerged from the front doors of the building, she was assailed with Texan and yellow rose imagery: "Outside the Alamo, Elizabeth was greeted by San Antonio's Winston Churchill High School band, playing 'The Eyes of Texas Are Upon You' and 'The Yellow Rose of Texas' as a young girl presented the queen one yellow rose" (*Washington Post*, May 22, 1991). The yellow rose is a metaphor for the Alamo itself—hybrid, as Emily Morgan.[5]

The structured past presented both in the museum exhibits and in the gardens also forms the basis of the two DRT-sponsored ceremonies at the Alamo. The larger and more public remembrance comes in the DRT's annual Pilgrimage to the Alamo. This ceremony is the means by which participants pay homage to the Alamo defenders before they indulge in the revelry of Fiesta. The pilgrimage began as an annual event in 1926, according to the history of Fiesta presented by the Institute of Texan Cultures. At its inception, the DRT organization sent invitations to participate in the pilgrimage to "dignitaries" within Texas, a practice which purportedly continues. These dignitaries include city and state officials as well as the president/chairman of all community organizations in the San Antonio area (e.g., Granaderos de Galvez, Girl Scouts, Texas Cavaliers). The representatives of local groups, many wearing uniforms of their organization, walk from the San Antonio Vietnam Memorial at the Municipal Auditorium to the Alamo, where they place floral arrangements, often having banners identifying the donor, on the grassy rectangle in front.

During this annual march from the Vietnam Memorial to the Alamo, an announcer inside the Alamo church calls the roll of the Alamo defenders, pronouncing each defender's name and place of origin. From the late 1960s onward this announcer has been Henry Guerra, who said (*mostly* in jest) that the DRT asked him to read the names since he could properly pronounce the Hispanic surnames of the Tejano defenders (Guerra 1988).

After all flowers have been presented, the Alamo Chapter conducts the remainder of the Pilgrimage to the Alamo ceremony. A minister of some Christian denomination offers an opening prayer, and then a DRT member explains the importance of the Alamo in Fiesta. She is followed by the president of the Fiesta Commission who offers a brief description of the meaning of Fiesta San Antonio and then introduces the main speaker, the Military Coordinator of Fiesta. After the Military Coordinator has completed his speech, the minister offers a closing prayer, and trumpeters play "Taps." In the eyes of the inside Alamo groups (i.e., the DRT, the Battle of Flowers

Association, the Texas Cavaliers, and the Order of the Alamo), homage has been paid, and revelry can begin.

The Pilgrimage to the Alamo is "open to the public," but the grandstands immediately in front of the Alamo are reserved for "special guests," many of which are military officers in full dress uniform. The dress of the pilgrimage "special guests" differs markedly from that of the special guests attending the Battle of Flowers Parade. As a solemn event within Fiesta week, the Pilgrimage to the Alamo contains the inversions of dress (solemn as opposed to festive) and of the direction of approach (south as opposed to north).

The most striking inversion during the pilgrimage is the least visible one: the Anglo women (DRT Alamo Chapter members) who are normally inside the Alamo walls are outside, and a Hispanic man (Guerra) is inside.

The tone of the Pilgrimage to the Alamo emphasizes both the inversion within it and the requirement that "the faithful" pay homage before entering into the festive mode. During the time of Fiesta, the faithful must remember the source of their privilege. The DRT speech offered at the 1989 pilgrimage stressed this point:

> Today we honor once again the heroes of the Alamo with this impressive floral offering and with participation of numerous community organizations and dedicated individuals; we pay tribute here in front of this shrine, this humble building, that has become a universal symbol of courage and dedication to the cause of freedom and dignity.

> (1989 Pilgrimage to the Alamo)

This debt relationship with the Alamo defenders was reiterated in the speech by the Military Coordinator of Fiesta of 1989:

> "Remember the Alamo." There is no clearer clarion call to commitment, no more succinct statement of sacrifice, no brighter beacon of brotherhood than those three words. . . . The heroes of the Alamo were the sons and grandsons of soldiers who fought in America's great war of independence. They had learned at the family table that freedom is never free, and that when it is threatened, each generation must realize that there is a price to be paid.

> (1989 Pilgrimage to the Alamo)

The honor given at the pilgrimage is an offering made to those who have paid the price for what people associated with the Alamo enjoy. Although this military officer declares that the Alamo and the saying "Remember the Alamo" represent brotherhood, he claims that the Alamo defenders descended from soldiers who fought in the American Revolution, thus excluding from this image of the heroes the Tejano defenders. Whether or not this exclusion is intentional, it is a common one.[6]

The Pilgrimage to the Alamo is the DRT's public call to the community leaders to acknowledge the importance of the Alamo's past. The Daughters' memorial service on March 6 is much more private; it is held inside the Alamo church and thus has very limited seating. Invitations go out to DRT members and special guests. If any seats remain, a few people outside the Daughters and their guests are allowed to come in. As very few seats are ever left, the service is, essentially, closed to the public except as viewed in televised clips in the local news. The DRT's enclosure inside the Alamo walls on the day of death again suggests unique connections with the Alamo heroes; seats are reserved for "the family."[7]

In the ceremonies at the Alamo the DRT makes clear what is meant by honoring the heroes and which heroes are the focus. The March 6 memorial service is conducted as a religious ceremony within a church rather than a historic site. For the 1990 service, a DRT member began by reminding those present that this was a memorial service and so they were not to applaud at any point. A Methodist minister gave an invocation, after which the DRT chaplain read Psalm 100. Then the president of the Children of the Republic of Texas read a poem eulogizing, in particular, Travis, Crockett, Bowie, and Bonham. This reading was followed by a roll call of states and nations represented by the Alamo defenders and an indication of the number of defenders from that nation or state. The 1990 service concluded with songs sung by a local choral group and the playing of "Taps."

The "special guest" status of the DRT for this ceremony on the battle anniversary accentuates the Alamo heir imagery of the organization projected throughout the year in literature distributed by the DRT and in their administration of the site. The Alamo appears as the inherited domain of DRT members, whose "ownership" is enforced outside by the Alamo Rangers. Their enclosure of themselves within the boundaries of state property gives the DRT an image of being firmly rooted as the authority figure at the site, and the members carefully guard their control of the site from those who would question the DRT's right to the hallowed ground.

The most frequent challenges to the DRT's authority at the Alamo come, not surprisingly, from Hispanics in San Antonio. As a result, some San Antonians see the DRT members as unduly harassed by the Hispanic community leaders. When city councilwoman Helen Ayala scolded the DRT for not helping fund a 1993 archaeological excavation, one San Antonian, Max C. Johnson, declared that the encounter was "nothing more than a person of Mexican descent who is belittling a group of old white women whose main objective is to preserve the memory of the event leading to the defeat of the Mexicans" (*San Antonio Express-News*, October 20, 1993). In this comment the DRT members appear as innocent and harmless matrons trying to keep the dust off of historical figures and events.

But when the matronly veneer is stripped away, another image of the DRT organization emerges. The DRT has controlled the site for almost ninety years, and members seem unwilling to surrender any of their authority without a major fight; when their authority is challenged, many of the DRT members turn combative. A cartoon by John Branch, printed during the controversy over the new IMAX film *Alamo . . . The Price of Freedom*, aptly portrays this tendency of the DRT (challenged, in this instance, by the League of United Latin American Citizens). The feeling in Branch's cartoon is that those who would attack the DRT's authority at the site are in for a tough fight with some die-hard old Texas women (Fig. 7.3).

Depending on the situation, DRT may be a group of quiet, matronly caretakers, properly using their brooms to keep the "house" in order; or they may be a crowd of angry battle-axes, swinging at all who question their authority. The DRT's ability to foster both the matron and the battle-ax images may well be partly responsible for its retention as the Alamo's custodian for over eighty years, despite its controversial interpretation of its past.

Part of the DRT's success in switching images lies in the popular perception of the Alamo as inconsequential in everyday life. In this view of the site, the women of the DRT, as part of the nonprofit, "private" sector, are not doing anything of economic or political importance inside the state-owned boundaries. Although the DRT does not support an image of the Alamo as inconsequential in everyday life, many of the members do foster an image of the Alamo as a women's (versus men's) domain. Their care of the site is given, in their words, "lovingly," and they have domesticated the Alamo with "cradle" and "home" images throughout their tenure. A 1959 DRT in-house letter refers to the Alamo as the house and its administration as housekeeping. This is woman's domain. Here, supposedly,

Fig. 7.3. Cartoon by John Branch.
*Reprinted by permission of John Branch.*

people (i.e., the heroes) are important, not money; here the past is purportedly the focus, not the future.

The quiet, nonbusiness character often awarded the DRT's administration of the Alamo has kept the issue of how much money the organization makes at the site out of the public eye for most of the DRT's custodianship. The Alamo and the DRT are not perceived primarily in business terms. As the product of a nonprofit enterprise, the finances at the Alamo may have appeared in the past as "home economics," relatively private and low scale. These "daughters," it *seemed*, performed their duty not for money but out of love.

Although this image of domestic femininity has protected the DRT from having to make public for over eighty years the amount of money received through the donation boxes and the gift shop, and how that money was being used, the femininity shield took a serious blow in 1988 when State Representative Orlando Garcia discovered that the DRT had $1.7 million in reserve and an annual budget of more than $1 million. After the initial questioning by Garcia, State Representative Jerry Beauchamp joined the probe, demanding to see the DRT's reports filed with the Internal Revenue Service. In response to this invasion, the DRT members verbally held these men at a distance until they could determine if they could deny them access to DRT financial records.

While the DRT was gathering its defenses, member Peggy Dibrell said, "We don't know anything about government rules, but we're willing to do anything we're told we have to do," thus assuming a "feminine" ignorance of outside public regulations. Furthermore, the DRT appeared childlike and ready to be obedient to the proper authority (the State of Texas or the federal government). This image of nonaggressive ignorance left Beauchamp, at least temporarily, in a "polite stand-off with the DRT" (*San Antonio Express-News*, November 16, 1988). This feminine image may well have bought the DRT time to prepare for the public eye its financial records in relation to the Alamo, or it may have been a testing of how much exemption the DRT organization commands in its role as custodian of the Alamo and as representative of powerful men, both living and dead.

Despite the DRT's claim to be giving attention to the Alamo out of "love," the way in which the DRT wields its authority at the site is increasingly coming into focus, with resulting tensions. DRT members, in the above scenario, play the role of deferring women (at least deferring to the "proper authority"). But in other situations, they often refuse to play such a role. In 1993, the DRT raised the ire of the then–mayor pro tem of San Antonio William Thornton when he, along with "Keep Texas Beautiful" officials from Austin, were forced off the state property at Alamo Plaza and into the street for a photography session, with the explanation that no commercial photos were allowed on state property. (Thornton had received the Governor's Community Achievement Award for environmental and recycling efforts, and the photograph being taken, with the Alamo as background, was for a slide to be shown at the annual "Keep Texas Beautiful" meeting in Austin.) After being evicted from state property by an Alamo Ranger, Thornton asked to see someone in charge. He refused to go inside the Alamo and left before any DRT members came out. Thornton demanded an apology from the DRT over the embarrassing eviction, and in reply the Alamo Committee chairwoman Anna Hartman telephoned Thornton and apologized for the confusion, but explained, "Rules are rules." Most unsatisfied, Thornton ordered a review of all recent and proposed city land deals with the DRT.

This rejection of a city official from the site raised several eyebrows, but many other rejections of various visitors, most notably the rejection of protestors, have not caused such a stir. It appears to be the accepted "law" that when protestors set foot on the state-owned Alamo property, they open themselves up to forceful removal by the Alamo Rangers, who under the direction of the DRT, remove anyone not behaving in the DRT-prescribed manner. Anyone who wishes to verbally attack the Alamo imagery and/or the DRT's use of the Alamo must do so on city property—"out in the street"— where the DRT has no control.

The limits of the DRT's control were tested immediately before the 1991 Pilgrimage to the Alamo. Three protestors claiming to be members of the Revolutionary Communist Youth Brigade approached the Alamo from the south (the direction from which the pilgrimage participants would soon arrive) carrying a red flag and chanting "Presente! Presente! Damian está presente! Con él! Con él! Con él está la gente!" [Damian is present. With him are the people]. They carried flowers which they declared were in memory of Damian Garcia, a man the protestors claimed was murdered by police agents in Los Angeles in 1980 because he was a revolutionary. (Garcia had, at some time in the past, climbed on the roof of the Alamo and raised "the red flag of revolution.") The protestors stopped in front of the Alamo and made a speech, first in English and then in Spanish, decrying the racism they felt was associated with the Alamo and its role in the creation of Texas. Throughout their presentation, an Alamo Ranger stood on the curb behind them, ensuring that they stayed on city property. When the protestors had finished their speech and were attempting to walk up to the church to present the flowers, they were stopped by the Alamo Ranger, who refused to allow them to set foot on the state property. They placed the flowers on the curb and then marched off chanting.[8]

No protest of the Alamo as symbol is allowed on the ground controlled by the DRT. Any ceremony or presentation must have DRT approval before occurring on this property. Such control exists for *all* events, even those honoring the Alamo heroes. When I asked DRT members and a DRT employee about the ceremonies held in front of the Alamo property (e.g., This Hallowed Ground and other ceremonies and religious services performed by various groups in San Antonio), I was told that these ceremonies were held "out in the street," a description which casts an aspersion on the legitimacy of these productions by outsiders.

The tensions between the outsiders and insiders of the Alamo are particularly strong during Fiesta when special privilege becomes explicit. Since the Texas Cavaliers and the Order of the Alamo are the only groups allowed to hold private ceremonies inside the church

and on its state-owned grounds, other groups and other Fiesta royalty must look elsewhere for their social reproduction. This exclusivity for some within San Antonio society has festered as a sore
spot. The Daughters are well aware of the tensions around them.
The ground they control is an island in a city teeming with the disenfranchised kin; every year, the protesting band around the Alamo
grows larger and more irritated.

# Chapter 8. Rejected Suitors

The Daughters of the Republic of Texas are the protective custodians who turn away from the Alamo people who they feel would misuse "the cradle of Texas liberty." Anyone allowed private use of this shrine must supply the Alamo with a meaning of the past condoned by the DRT; the society that annually renews itself in the stone womb must be avowedly "Texan."

But being avowedly Texan is not all that the DRT requires, and the organization often denies requests from various groups who wish to use the Alamo for private functions. When the prestigious Cattle Barons association requested special use of the Alamo in 1990, the DRT denied it. A DRT member wrote to the executive director of the Texas Historical Commission to ask for his support of the DRT's refusal to grant this request on the grounds that the function was less than reverent, with Willie Nelson as the entertainment. She claimed that the pressure she felt in denying this request exceeded any she had experienced before in her administrative position at the Alamo. Many of the Cattle Barons are socially prominent in San Antonio, and they, according to this DRT member, feel that they should be allowed to do as they wish at the Alamo.

This particular rejection reveals that the DRT does *not* base denial of requests solely on ethnicity or social status. This type of rejection (that is, of socially prominent Anglos) will not hit the newspapers, nor will it spark public protest. But if the rejection does *appear* to be based on ethnicity, the anger becomes public. Protests performed on Alamo Plaza almost invariably involve the Anglo-versus-Hispanic imagery in San Antonio. The Alamo provides the favorite arena for declaring social exclusion and for decrying the enemy image of Hispanics in historical accounts, and the DRT often serves as target for this anger.

Several Hispanic social and political leaders in San Antonio claim

that the DRT's production of the Alamo's past pushes out most Hispanics, who are, in their eyes, the legitimate heirs to this popular
tourist attraction. Many feel that their ancestors (therefore, they)
have been displaced in the past portrayed at the site. John Leal, archivist at the Bexar County Courthouse, expresses the anger some
Hispanics feel toward this displacement:

> The Alamo belongs to the state; it doesn't belong to the Daugh-
> ters. I have the contract here. They don't *own* it; they're only
> care-takers. . . . They didn't pay for the buildings or the grounds.
> *We*, the citizens, with our tax money that went into the state,
> my ancestors, my grandfather, my father's taxes, paid for that
> land. So I have a right, as a descendant. . . . So right away they
> take possession of what's not theirs. Little do they realize they
> can be replaced by the state, . . . whether they continue to . . .
> give false information and not the truth. . . . They don't want the
> story to come out that there was something here before 1836. . . .
> We've been erased. We've been cut out. We don't exist. And that's
> why we protest. They're trying to erase us, and we refuse to be
> erased.
>
> (Leal 1988)

In this view, the Daughters are only caretakers, more similar to
groundskeepers than guardians. But, according to Leal, they pretend
to be owners through inheritance; the true owners are people such
as himself whose ancestors paid taxes.[1]

John Leal typifies the people within San Antonio who want to
rework the past presented at the Alamo and its role in the beginnings of San Antonio to include Hispanics, the "erased" people. In
their eyes, this exclusion is not simply neglectful; it is malicious.
Leal does not decry the *use* of a creation myth, but the lack of an
important and desirable role for Hispanics in the current story line.

Such identity comes in names, both of groups and of individuals.
Leal's business card exemplifies this means of establishing identity:

John O. Leal
Bexar County Archivist
Canary Island Descendant
A Hidalgo of Texas
Granadero de Galvez
Son of the Republic of Texas

These titles depend on ancestors (except "archivist," which denotes a connection to the past via occupation, and "Granadero de Galvez," a group which, though sounding ancestral, is open to the public). Leal declares his ancestors to have been Canary Islanders and nobility (*hidalguia*). The nobility claim is an appendage to the Canary Island distinction; in 1731, the king of Spain, Philip V, granted the nobility status of *hidalgo* to all male Canary Islanders settling in Tejas, and that nobility was supposed to be passed down to descendants. Thus *hidalguia* is an identity of Spanish nobility, then and now, in a purportedly Mexican town. The status of these forefathers in San Antonio society has been erased, in Leal's perspective, by the current Alamo mythology and the DRT's overall Anglo, as opposed to Spanish/Mexican, emphasis.

Leal and other people claiming *hidalguia* differentiate between the Spanish and the Mexican heritages of the region for status purposes; they are the *España* Hispanics of San Antonio. Many San Antonians, however, do not make this distinction, but group all Hispanics into the Mexican American category. Although the official history distributed by the DRT at the Alamo allocates separate roles to the two nationalities, some of the DRT members, in their comments about Hispanics in San Antonio, neglect the distinction.

But the distinction is also of little importance to many of the city's Hispanics with Mexican-born parents. A local history professor, Gilbert Hinojosa, feels that the Canary Island descendants "lost their 'Spanishness' very quickly because numbers are destiny, and there weren't enough of them for the next generation . . . to marry one another" (Hinojosa 1988). According to this viewpoint, there is no ethnic superiority of the Canary Island descendants because there is no physical distinction. Hinojosa has been one of the most active Hispanic community leaders, both in person and in print, in efforts to give Hispanics—particularly those with Mexican ancestry—an audible voice in San Antonio's legacy. Defining numbers as destiny, Hinojosa claims that it is the influx of Mexicans after the turn of the twentieth century that has caused the Anglo mythology to be questioned and to ask who had been in Texas before the Anglos; in such a viewpoint, it is primarily the Mexican descendants, not the Spanish ones, who are pressing the sociopolitical levers in San Antonio and demanding a rewriting of popular history at the Alamo.

In the eyes of Hinojosa and others proud of the Mexican American category, the problem becomes how to rewrite the myth to include Hispanics for the sake of the Mexican descendants who now compose such a large part of the San Antonio population. He, and others protesting the movie *Alamo . . . The Price of Freedom*, felt that the producers ignored an opportunity to make a film which represented the current demographics of the region:

Time was right for a new version of the epic simply because an epic, while it is set in the past, is meant to say something about the present. . . . Many of us have had the myth used against us, and to that extent there is a resentment [against] the myth.

(Hinojosa 1988)

Hinojosa explained that many Hispanic children growing up in Texas have feared the seventh grade, for at that age they have been told that the Mexicans were "the bad guys" who killed David Crockett and the other Alamo heroes. The mythology creates an "immigrant" status for the Hispanics in which the "immigrants" feel as though they are under siege or attack (Hinojosa 1988). From seventh grade on, Hispanics in Texas have received an unwanted kinship with the enemies of the past.

Creating kinship, both with antagonists and with heroes, becomes clear in the protest some Hispanics staged on the evening of the IMAX film's premiere. Gilbert Hinojosa and others formed a picket line outside the theater. Hinojosa called the roll of the nine Tejano defenders over and over, with the rest of the protestors crying "Presente!" after each name. He and the Hispanics around him declared a presence for the Tejanos embodied in living Hispanics; they assumed an identity with and a descendancy from these historic figures inside the Alamo.

But Hinojosa, unlike many people who contend kinship with the site, recognized the created descendancy. He watched Reynaldo Esparza, a descendant of a Tejano defender, cross the picket line along with DRT members, the film producers, the governor of Texas, and other special guests to go inside the theater. Hinojosa then looked around at all the sons and daughters of immigrants standing near him and realized he had no kinship via bloodlines with the names he called; anyone who does *and who accepts the conventional history of the site* is already part of the "in" group (Hinojosa 1990).

Hinojosa understands that the kinship he declared with the Tejano defenders is based on ethnicity, on having Hispanic surnames and having relatives who at one time or another were Mexican citizens (Hinojosa 1990). These are the same grounds on which he and other Hispanics receive kinship with "the enemy." The descendancy they would take is not that which they receive in the Alamo mythology.

In this light, Hinojosa places Reynaldo Esparza with the inside group because Esparza, as a descendant of the Tejano Alamo defender Gregorio Esparza, has an identity in the Alamo past complete with ancestors and birth certificates. His inclusion among the guests for the film's premiere lends legitimacy to the film and an illegitimacy to the declared kinship of "sons and daughters of immigrants" standing outside without invitations.

But Hinojosa is making a distinction between Hispanics inside and Hispanics outside that does not necessarily exist, at least not in the simple terms that it appears here. Reynaldo Esparza is himself a victim of his name. He is not always on the inside, nor is there particular comfort in being a Tejano defender's descendant, according to his experiences. Esparza claims that his Hispanic surname and his descendancy leave him "a man without an identity" in San Antonio. Although he likes to call himself a Tejano, he doesn't feel comfortable using that distinction around other Hispanics in San Antonio who might think he is "putting on airs." Nor does he feel at ease calling himself an American around other Hispanics who might prefer the term Chicano or Mexican. Even in Anglo company he is not fully "American"; he feels that upon hearing "Esparza," Anglos think "Mexican," finding the Spanish language of his name alien (Esparza 1988). Thus, one of the most personal and identifying possessions of his famous ancestors—the Spanish language— disenfranchises this native son.

Esparza is cautious in his use of Spanish, choosing not to speak Spanish in public:

I'm not exactly excommunicating myself from the language or the Spanish heritage. . . . That is still in me, but not primarily. . . . I love the language, but I don't go around carrying on conversations. . . . I think we'd be put in a foreigner category if we go around speaking Spanish in mixed company. What the kickers would make of that! . . . I'm very discreet when I'm using my Spanish.

(Esparza 1988)

The Spanish language, a personal love Esparza feels some people will use to justify discrimination, becomes a privacy-only birthmark.

Anglos are not alone in finding the Spanish language foreign. Spanish is the language best forgotten in the eyes of some Hispanics, especially in the eyes of a child entering the school system. One Hispanic community leader working with the Guadalupe Cultural Arts Center, Juan Tejeda, said that his elementary school–aged nephew corrected him for speaking Spanish, saying that "English is better." Tejeda feels that the built-in racism in the school system is responsible for his nephew's rejection of Spanish (Tejeda 1988). This rejection of Spanish in favor of English appears widespread in this region. According to Nef Garcia, a political science professor who once ran for public office, about 95 percent of Hispanics in San Antonio prefer English to Spanish, and a comparable percentage do not know how to write Spanish (Garcia 1989). As Esparza's use of Spanish suggests, it is a language usually reserved in San Antonio for private conversation.

Esparza's difficulty with identity is typical of those who are sometimes inside and sometimes outside the Alamo mythology. He is a Tejano defender on the inside by descendancy, but a Mexican American to the unknowing by virtue of his Hispanic surname and his residence on the west side of town. Although on paper he is a blood relative of early Texas and his ancestor's blood was spilled inside the Alamo, his supposed ethnicity disowns him. Esparza's kinship and claim to the Alamo are invisible to most San Antonians. What is visible is his ethnicity, which, in the current mythology, erases his inheritance.

Thus people claiming Hispanic heritage face an insider/outsider dichotomy, which becomes the basis for tension within some of the Hispanic organizations in San Antonio. This dichotomy creates tension within individuals who involve themselves with the business and politics of the city; the question becomes, Who are we, and what is ours? Gilbert Hinojosa discovered the division on a personal level when he stood outside and watched other Hispanics go inside the IMAX film premiere. But the division has affected Hispanic political groups as well. Nef Garcia described this tension within the Hispanic organization League of United Latin American Citizens:

LULAC is broken up into at least two camps: One camp is very pragmatic, almost nonideological, almost business oriented; and the other is more socially oriented, more political. And that dichotomy has always created a level of tension in LULAC. [The pragmatic camp would say,] "Let's mainstream, let's all become Americans." . . . Assimilation is well on its way. The only differ-

ence is that we're so affected by the international border, being
so close to it, that we are in constant nourishment of our culture.
So we're in effect leading two cultural lives.

(Garcia 1989)

According to Garcia, a LULAC member is in either one camp or the
other, depending on his or her emphasis on business or sociopolitical gains for the membership. But the external splitting into camps
is echoed within the individual member who is by definition and
preferred language American, yet who feels "nourished" socially by
Mexico. In this perspective, "Culture" confronts "culture"; Mexico
is the mother country and the perceived culture source which births
and nourishes the Hispanic, whereas the United States is the male
business world that pulls the Hispanic away from home.

This male/female opposition of the United States and Mexico
and thus of Anglo versus Hispanic had its beginning in the nineteenth century. A particularly poignant example of this ideology appears in the writing of a governor of Texas during the later 1800s,
Oran Roberts, who denigrated Mexican masculinity and praised its
femininity:

With their [the Mexican] standard of manhood, and arts of war,
the struggle with the wild savages was long, and often doubt-
ful in maintaining their position in the country. That difficulty,
perhaps, contributed largely to their invitation of the Anglo-
Americans to share with them their lands and dangers; which,
commencing formally in 1821, resulted in establishing numerous
colonies for the settlement of white men. The antagonism of
races soon commenced, and was kept up from various grounds,
until the Anglo-Americans, by the aid of some noble Mexicans,
remained masters of the field. . . . The Mexicans are now re-
duced to small numbers in a few localities. They have left behind
them one stone-house in eastern Texas; . . . one town in western
Texas, San Antonio, now a delightful city, the Bagdad of America; also in the west, the wreck of some stone-built Missions of
the olden time, and one mule path, called formerly the "King's
highway." . . . They have left with us the art of throwing a rope
in catching animals, and some other arts of stock raising and
training. . . . They have left their names of rivers, and creeks, and
of some counties and towns. . . . And they have left, lingering in
the memory of many an old Texan, the universal Christian char-
ity and humanity of the Mexican women, who were ever ready to

feed, to comfort, and to plead for mercy towards the Texan prisoner in time of war.

(Roberts 1881:20–21)

The Mexican male, according to the mythological categories displayed in the above passage, is lacking in manhood, measured in his
ability to create order out of chaos in taming the wilderness; his low
technology in the "arts of war" makes him less a man than the Anglo American who will become the master of the field. What is of
value in the Mexican culture, according to the mythology, is the
feminine *nature* of the culture. The Mexican women, with their
aura of religious grace and mothering, are praiseworthy; the men,
unable to properly settle the region, are not worthy to be among the
bearers of Culture who become the masters of the field. The Mexican man's feeble attempts at civilization appear as singular achievements (i.e., one noteworthy house) or are denigrated to the status of
nature (i.e., their "King's highway" is a "mule path"). Otherwise, the
achievements of the Mexican man are primarily, according to the
mythology, in relation to nature (i.e., catching animals and naming
rivers) rather than civilization.

The ideological dichotomy offered by Roberts remains alive in the
current debilitating split within LULAC itself and within individuals, but few recognize the mythologized nature/culture split or the
Culture/culture opposition. The question becomes, what do people
in San Antonio (and the entire nation) mean by "the two cultures."
Garcia speaks of two cultures—nourishing country versus adopted
nationality—warring within himself, but he also speaks of the two
cultures as distinct racial categories based on skin tone when he
makes note of a cartoon tabloid produced by the Socony-Mobil Oil
Company during the 1950s:

That little cartoon tabloid affected all of our generation. . . . That
[tabloid] pretty much established the parameters of the relationship between browns and whites in Texas and San Antonio for
generations.

(Garcia 1989)[2]

From one dichotomy springs another, sectioning off individuals
and groups into sharply contrasted identities. When the divisions
occur internally, the group and the individual lose the strength of
conviction, such as the division among local Hispanic historians
during the filming of *Alamo . . . The Price of Freedom*. The movie's

producers, aware of the ethnic tension within San Antonio, arranged a meeting of Hispanic community leaders. Several of the Hispanics voiced concern over how the film would treat Hispanics, thus expressing the sociopolitical aspect. Felix Almaraz, one of the people questioning the producers, was one of the least combative, asking primarily who was to be the protagonist and who was to serve as antagonist in the story line. He was later asked by the producers to serve as "cultural consultant." After Almaraz accepted this role on the production staff, those Hispanics who continued to protest had less public ground.

Almaraz becomes the Hispanic inside, participating in production. But he is also within the category of "Hispanic historians," a category in which stand others who denounce the story line, such as Richard Santos. During the production of the film, Santos sent commentaries through the press to incite the Hispanic community to what he felt to be rightful rage over the story line's built-in racism. Nef Garcia explained that these two Hispanic historians— Almaraz and Santos—represent the business/sociopolitical dichotomy within LULAC (a conflict that exists, too, within many individuals). When asked where Henry Guerra (the voice inside the Alamo during the DRT's Pilgrimage to the Alamo) fits on the spectrum, Garcia declared that Guerra stands "as the unblemished Spaniard who is above the fray" (Garcia 1989).

Guerra, in contrast to Reynaldo Esparza, is an outsider brought inside the Alamo by the DRT and by his locally broadcast vignettes of Texas history. Guerra is so closely tied to the Alamo image that he began an interview by saying "It is incorrect to suppose that I was at the battle of the Alamo. No, I wasn't" (Guerra 1988). Guerra does not claim to be a Canary Island descendant since his ancestors did not arrive until 1749, but he takes pride in being Hispanic, and enjoys pointing out the early mixed marriages (Anglo male to Hispanic female). His own feelings are that Travis was anti-Mexican; yet Guerra takes pride in the Alamo story as one of "devotion to a cause" and counts himself among the "we" of the Texans losing at the Alamo and winning at San Jacinto (Guerra 1988).

Nef Garcia, in placing Guerra above the fray, introduces yet another facet to the divided Hispanic image: the Spaniard who is not a Canary Islander. The distinction declares a more tolerated social legitimacy (i.e., a less competitive claim) *if* the individual making this Hispanic ancestry claim does not alienate prestigious Anglo groups.

Henry Guerra is able to avoid that social pitfall, remaining aloof from the sociopolitical struggles within San Antonio; when asked his opinion on controversial issues, he responds diplomatically and conservatively. When asked by San Antonio radio personality Alan Dale where Jeff Long had "gone wrong" in his controversial book *Duel of Eagles*, Guerra offered a balanced response:

> I'm not sure he went wrong. . . . Take a look at the title: it says "Duel of Eagles" and then it says "The Mexican and U.S. fight for the Alamo." That's correct, to a certain extent. In other words, for the first time this is an acknowledgement . . . in English that the United States had a lot to do with the Texas Revolution. . . . However, I can't agree with all of his conclusions. I think he has, in trying to bring about a true picture, . . . overreached somewhat. I cannot look upon the men who fought and died at the Alamo as a bunch of adventurers who were out only for personal gain. . . . We are beginning to find material that was not available twenty or thirty or fifty years ago to the historians of that day. And I think we did go a little overboard in worshiping the heroes of the Alamo. Nonetheless, you can't take away the historical fact that a group of men, who were vastly outnumbered, gave their lives for the cause they believed in. They chose to die fighting for that cause. I think that's still the basic story of the Alamo: a story of real heroism.
>
> (Guerra 1990b)

Alan Dale then acknowledges that what Guerra has presented is really two viewpoints, one that questions the conventional history and another that supports it. Yet Guerra ends by supporting "the basic story" of the Alamo, declaring that it is still valid. In this manner, Guerra refuses to take sides in this controversy and exemplifies his position "above the fray" of social and political tensions between Anglos and Hispanics.

Few Hispanics can maintain such a position; in their attempts to claim an identity within San Antonio's established society, the majority find themselves supporting either the business accommodation or the sociopolitical anger, which together form the internal struggle for an individual. These two forces are antithetical. The Hispanic who would claim San Antonio's past as contained in the Alamo must simultaneously declare and deny the validity of its mythology which lauds the productive Anglo's arrival. Some politically active Hispanics, such as Gilbert Hinojosa and Nef Garcia, recognize their dilemma; but many seem unaware of the internal dialogue they carry into public displays.

This internal dialogue over "who are we and what is ours" plagues Hispanics caring to claim a part of this first Hispanic mission in

South Texas, this number-one tourist attraction in the state, and this international icon of sacrifice. Its Anglo-order-from-Mexican-chaos theme confronts Hispanics, dividing them as individuals and as groups, and setting them against themselves in the argument of what Hispanics want and how it can be gained.

This division allows some San Antonians to depict Hispanics as jealously squabbling among themselves, an image offered by one of my informants regarding a 1989 split within LULAC over the Rey Feo title. Of course, people claiming Hispanic heritage do not have the corner on the market for such internal struggles. The Alamo Chapter of the DRT, as of 1993, divided into two chapters after their own infighting. One DRT member (and others outside the organization) declared that Queen Elizabeth II's 1991 visit to the Alamo served as catalyst for the split, with DRT members in a "cat fight" with one another over proximity to the queen. And the early years of the Fiesta Commission showed such jealousies among the Anglo businessmen of the city, with Reynolds Andricks and other members of the Fiesta San Jacinto Association pitted against one another.

But when schism occurs within a "minority" group, discord appears as part of an innate and debilitating "nature." Chaotic characteristics (assigned, in this case, to Hispanics) appear as the reason for the group's "minority" status. Order comes from Anglos in the mythology, a concept that pervades the city, state, and nation; otherwise, it would not survive in the Alamo narratives.

With this emphasis on Anglo accomplishment within the story line, there are some Hispanic community leaders who want nothing whatsoever to do with the Texas creation mythology, at least not on the side of the Texans. One renowned Hispanic scholar refused initially to speak with me about the Alamo, saying it was too negative a symbol for Hispanics. After my pleading for an explanation, he declared that Hispanics should not glory in the Tejano defenders who fought inside the Alamo, for these Tejanos had been deceived by Sam Houston and Andrew Jackson; these Tejanos were fighting for a lie.

But people who do reject the Alamo entirely—not even wishing to discuss the topic—are few. Even those professing that the site cannot be made into a positive Hispanic image want to talk about the Alamo and the damage it has done Hispanics now living in Texas. The Alamo serves as a focal point for various groups to declare their exclusion from political power in the city, state, and nation.

The Alamo also serves as a ceremonial counterpoint; the fact that a particular ceremony is *not* at the Alamo has significance. The

most poignant example is the blessing of Rey Feo's crown, a "tradition" that started during the 1990 Fiesta San Antonio. The Rey Feo
who began the tradition, Sonny Melendrez, described its inception:

> This was not part of the [official Rey Feo] schedule. . . . We de-
> cided that on the first Sunday of Fiesta that we would go to nine
> o'clock mass at San Fernando [Cathedral]. Now that mass is tele-
> vised all over the world [every Sunday] . . . because there are so
> many Spanish-speaking countries. San Fernando Cathedral is
> very well known—it's incredible the history that lies there. . . .
> Before we went into the church, Father Elizondo, who celebrates
> the mass, said, "Why don't we have you offer as [your gift to the
> altar] your crown." So I put my crown on the altar, and then he
> introduced everybody, of course—the entourage, etcetera. We
> had the mass, we had communion—everything. And at the end,
> before we walked out of the church with Father Elizondo, we
> went up to be introduced again and then to get the crown, and he
> [Bishop Flores] was going to hand it back to me. Well, it just hap-
> pened, it just felt that what should be was that I should kneel
> down. And so as he went to hand me the crown, I knelt, and he
> crowned me.
>
> (Melendrez 1991)

This crowning by a real bishop in a real cathedral rivals the crowning of King Antonio in front of the Alamo. Both sites are historic
landmarks, both are favorite sites for the media, and both crownings
have large audiences.

One curious coincidence lies in Santa Anna's having flown the red
flag signaling no quarter for the 1836 Alamo defenders from the bell
tower of San Fernando Cathedral. The "rightness" of this new tradition, begun in the most imposing symbol of the Hispanic past and
presence within San Antonio, reveals the growing division within
San Antonio society during Fiesta. The strong symbolic importance
of the sites chosen for social rebirth magnifies the feeling of exclu-
sion/inclusion during this time in which San Antonio groups are
supposed to unite.

According to some historians of Fiesta, the Rey Feo position itself
grew out of this feeling of exclusion from the Anglo group the Texas
Cavaliers and its King Antonio. Jack Maguire declares that the claim
by LULAC that their Fiesta king's selection is inclusive rather than
exclusive is "an obvious barb at the Cavaliers' tradition of always
choosing one of their own" (Maguire 1990:55). Whether or not the

Rey Feo position grew out of an animosity Hispanics felt about King Antonio's Anglo origin, some Hispanics in the last few decades have openly questioned the Texas Cavaliers' exclusivity. In 1983, when one of the Texas Cavaliers, Bill Watson, was asked whether there would ever be a Hispanic King Antonio, Watson replied:

> Many of us have Hispanic friends but I don't know if they'd want to be Cavaliers. But if the time ever came, I would choose people whom I thought would work hard and do a job well. I don't always vote for my friends when I don't think they can handle the job.
>
> (*San Antonio Light*, April 17, 1983)

In this statement, Watson points out that there are very few Hispanics in the Texas Cavaliers (at last count, only one), and certainly none in a position to vie for the role of King Antonio.

By creating the Rey Feo position, the division between Anglos and Hispanics during Fiesta has come more into focus, and some who have held these positions of Fiesta royalty try either to deny or to counteract this division. Former Rey Feo Logan Stewart declared that "there would be no Rey Feo Parade during Fiesta Week if we hadn't received the total support of the Texas Cavaliers from the very start. They have been with us all the way" (*San Antonio Express-News*, November 12, 1984).

But this support may well stem from the Texas Cavaliers' desire to lessen the social pressure for their group to admit people of other ethnic groups, for there are only three Jewish, one Hispanic, and no Black members (out of more than four hundred Texas Cavaliers). A writer for *Texas Monthly* addressed this issue in his study of King Antonio:

> Inevitably, the Cavaliers fall back on their old standby: they remind other organizations that each organization is free to elect its own Fiesta king and add that they themselves welcome as many as the public will allow. . . . In 1980 LULAC Council Two got its king, the Rey Feo, into Fiesta on an equal basis with Antonio.
>
> (T. Walker 1983:217)

Even if the two kings have equal visibility to the public now, there remain tensions between the two groups. Although one former Rey Feo declared his strong friendship with the King Antonio of his Fiesta reign, he expressed his irritation at the lack of reciprocity within the "traditional" invitations: King Antonio is invited to a reception for Rey Feo, but Rey Feo is not invited to King Antonio's reception. Despite the staged embraces between the two kings throughout Fiesta, the underlying feeling is that true equality does not exist.

The official, "traditional" opening of Fiesta attempts to deny this inequality and division by having both Rey Feo and King Antonio in front of the Alamo cracking a giant *cascarone* (a confetti-filled egg). Although this site is a focal point for celebrations in which both kings appear as vessels of the southwestern "traditions," it is also where feelings of exclusion are, according to some Hispanics, exceedingly powerful. Nef Garcia feels that "in very subtle ways, the Alamo still perpetuates that legacy of antagonism, . . . the legacy of hate between the two cultures" (Garcia 1989).

This antagonism between two cultures as represented in the Texas Cavaliers and LULAC surfaces in unexpected ways. Garcia feels that one of the reasons the 1989 King Antonio and the rest of the Texas Cavaliers supported Rey Feo Nick Garza in a dispute with LULAC during the 1989 Fiesta was their desire to see the Hispanic organization divided against itself:

There's a reason why King Antonio took Rey Feo and said, "Come, you can share my barge [in the Texas Cavalier River Parade] if they don't let you ride on your barge." It wasn't because they're great buddies, but King Antonio saw an opportunity here to break with LULAC, further divide the two camps [the local chapter and the national organization].[3] And for some of us who saw the Rey Feo then embrace King Antonio in a kind of a paternalistic way, it didn't sit well with some of us.

(Garcia 1989)

Whether or not Stanton Bell was being opportunistic in his invitation, the feeling among some Hispanics is that the Texas Cavaliers would not willingly promote, and would even work subtly to undermine, the strength of a group, such as LULAC, that works for the empowerment of Hispanics.

Creating an image of San Antonio as a town shared by Hispanic and Anglo cultures, as attempted in joint appearances of Rey Feo and King Antonio, is one thing; actually sharing the town—socially, politically, and financially—is quite another. Any reclaiming of the Hispanic contributions to the past (and therefore inheritance rights in the present) comes slowly, having to push against the social categories defined in the Texas creation mythology.

One of the most subtle, yet penetrating ways to reaffirm Hispanic ancestry is through that same entity which many Hispanics feel must be reserved for private use: the Spanish language. Spanish names surface throughout the mythology, marking the places where sacred events occurred. The reclaiming of these sites begins in reclaiming the pronunciation of their names. The most apparent reclaiming occurs in how the name San Jacinto is pronounced. Unlike the English \j\, the Spanish "j" is aspirated, similar to the English \h\, and the Spanish "i" sounds like the English \ē\. But most public speakers saying the name of the battle site use an English pronunciation as opposed to the Spanish.

The Hispanic claims implicit in the Spanish pronunciation become more explicit when the English and Spanish pronunciations occur within the same ceremony, as happened during the 1989 Pilgrimage to the Alamo. The DRT member who served as master of ceremonies used the English pronunciation in her speech connecting Fiesta's origin as a commemoration of the Alamo heroes' sacrificial role in "buying time" for Sam Houston to become victorious at San Jacinto. In contrast, the next speaker, Roger Flores (who had received the conventional invitation to speak at the pilgrimage as president of the Fiesta Commission), used the Spanish pronunciation of San Jacinto in his speech in which he declared that Fiesta is a time for San Antonio to celebrate itself, focusing primarily on the city over time and its current population rather than on the birth of Texas (1989 Pilgrimage to the Alamo). In this way, Spanish pronunciation declares a legitimacy for the Hispanics within the region as a "we were here first" as well as a majority claim to the social climate.

Using the Spanish pronunciation also serves as a means of protest for anyone who wishes to declare a sympathetic unity with Hispanics, and/or who wishes to fire public salvos at the DRT and the Texas creation mythology. Such a use of the Spanish pronunciation of San Jacinto came from Jeff Long, author of the controversial book *Duel of Eagles: The Mexican and U.S. Fight for the Alamo*, in an interview conducted by radio personality Alan Dale. In the interview, Long claimed that the majority of the venerated Texas heroes at the Alamo and at San Jacinto were mercenaries interested in land to be gained rather than in moral principles; he attempted in the interview to shock the audience's expectations, both through his description of events and through his pronunciation of names. Long was only partially successful in his attempt to pronounce San Jacinto; he used the aspirated Spanish "j," but then muffed the Spanish "i," reverting to the short English \i\ (as in "pin"). Due to his linguistic error, he was unable to fully assume the image of the historian in possession of inside knowledge of the "natives."

However, Long's intended message in using the Spanish "j"—that Americans stole Mexican property in the taking/making of Texas— comes through clearly. In Long's version, Hispanics are the legitimate heirs of the region.

But critics such as Jeff Long are outnumbered within the United States and within Texas. The legitimate offspring appears to be, in the eyes of the public and by the arm of the law, the DRT; this organization controls who enters and who, in special circumstances, emerges from the front door (as opposed to the side exit) of this societal womb.[4] All those who would proclaim offspring of the Alamo *not* recognized in the DRT's presentation of the past must remain outside "in the street" to state their case.

Such a proclamation of other heirs was incorporated in a program sponsored in 1987 by the Catholic church. The Alamo church was the final focus in a "Music at the Missions" program which had highlighted each of the Spanish missions in San Antonio with a separate mass. The Catholic church was not given permission to perform a mass in the Alamo church, so the Catholic priest performing the ceremony held the mass outside of the building on city property. In his sermon, the priest declared that the other missions in San Antonio are "an expression of belief in and commitment to a God who loves, a God who saves." He contrasted the aura of these missions to that of the Alamo:

> But look at what has become of the humble church behind us. It is not even known to most people as Mission San Antonio, but around the world as the Alamo. It has become a shrine to a battle, a shrine to the actions of men. Its history has been distorted to demean and insult a people. The myths of the Alamo have wounded a group of Christian Texans. Let us, instead, celebrate Mission San Antonio by praising the God who inspired this church and pray that we might treat each other as *true daughters and sons*, brothers and sisters under our loving Father in Heaven [emphasis added].
>
> (*San Antonio Express-News*, June 20, 1987)

This priest decries the lost mission's new role in life as a secular shrine devoted to the actions of men. With this secular life comes false kinship, suggested in the appeal that the "we" of this congregation treat each other as *true* daughters and sons.

The above speech implies an ideological grouping of people within the community; the claim that the myths surrounding the Alamo "have wounded a group of Christian Texans" suggests simultaneously two groups: Hispanics and Catholics. These two distinctions are often conflated in San Antonio, allowing political and social battles at the Alamo to occur under religious terms. One of the more recent such battles occurred over a skull unearthed during a 1979 excavation within the compound's boundaries. The skull was primarily a curiosity, at least initially. From the military artifacts found near the skull, archaeologist Anne Fox determined that the skull was of a casualty of the 1836 battle. Somehow after the battle this body (or part of a body) had been overlooked in the rubble and was neither formally buried with the Mexican dead nor cremated with the Texans (it was impossible to determine on which side the person had fought). The skull was taken to the archaeology laboratory at the University of Texas at San Antonio for cleaning, analysis, and storage along with artifacts from the excavation.

But within a few years of its discovery, the skull was given to the DRT by the state archaeologist with the condition that the DRT provide proper storage for it in their library. In the remaining years the skull has been, quite literally, a bone of contention between the DRT and various organizations. One group, the William B. Travis Chapter of the Sons of the Republic of Texas, offered to build a tomb for the skull so that the alleged battle victim could have a "proper burial." The SRT began designing a tomb and memorial, complete with eternal flame (*Sherman Democrat*, August 11, 1985).

In another attempt four years later, a spokesperson for the Catholic church demanded during Fiesta 1989 that the skull be allowed a Christian burial as it was "a Roman Catholic skull" (*San Antonio Express-News*, April 12, 1989). The implicit understanding at this point was that the victim was undoubtedly part of the Mexican army. After considerable pressure from the Hispanic communities, the DRT voted to bury the skull in the Alamo compound, thus keeping it out of the domain of the Catholic church and, by extension, out of the hands of Hispanics.

Even this burial was not performed. Today the skull remains in a climate-controlled vault in the DRT Library. Keeping the skull in the library politically sterilizes it and keeps it from growing into a more visible symbol with its interment in the earth of the Alamo compound. If buried on city property, as had been suggested by the SRT, the skull's burial would give a site, owned and sanctioned by the city, for people to commemorate the casualties of the 1836

Alamo battle. What would be particularly odious for some of the DRT members is for the skull's supposed Mexican heritage to be stressed, thus creating a site where the Mexican dead could be commemorated.

The concern over a publicized, Christian burial of the skull proved too much for one DRT member, who protested, "The Catholics think it has to have a Catholic ceremony. We have nothing against a Christian burial, but the bodies of other people who died at the Alamo weren't given a Christian burial either" (*San Antonio Light*, April 20, 1989). The implication here is that the Alamo defenders were not given "a Christian burial," but were cremated in accord with Santa Anna's order. This reason for not burying the skull appears to be a tit-for-tat retaliation aimed at "Catholics" (i.e., Hispanics).

But this outburst by a DRT member was unusual. The DRT's *usual* approach to this topic, and other controversial issues, is silence; the less publicity, the better. They retain the skull on the inside of their domain, and access to the skull is very limited, as visitors must declare their purpose for being in the library before they are allowed to enter the main reading room. Even if someone wishing to venerate the skull were to obtain entrance to the library and then to the vault, his commemoration of the Mexican dead would have an extremely limited audience and thus no public impact.

The skull and association with it remain out of Hispanic control, even though it presumably belonged to a Mexican man. However, one of the more vocal Hispanic community leaders, Robert Benavides, has—ironically—managed to become closely associated with the bones of an Anglo hero. In 1993 the remains of Ben Milam were exhumed after Benavides directed researchers to Milam's most probable burial site. The press releases on the exhumation pointed to Benavides as the reason Milam's bones were not forever lost.

But Milam's remains, a hundred years earlier, had been the focus of another Hispanic community leader, Adina De Zavala. According to records of her life, De Zavala had been active in the preservation of Milam's grave during the 1890s. John Leal, a close friend of Benavides, sent me a photocopy of a 1933 article, appearing in the *San Antonio Light*, in which Adina De Zavala placed a wreath in Milam Park on the grave of Ben Milam to commemorate the heroes of the Texas Revolution, an act she performed on the anniversary of the Alamo battle. In his note accompanying the article he sent me, Leal wrote: "This was the only thing available to honor the fallen heroes of Texas of 1836. Now Milam is [the] forgotten hero of 1836 during the taking of S.A. from Gen. Cos in Dec. Times sure change with years" (Leal 1990).

Part of the intrigue in Milam's remains may stem from his *not* being one of the Alamo casualties. Furthermore, Ben Milam's sacrifice—which occurred in December 1835—preceded the Alamo's fall, much as the Hispanics preceded the Anglos in this region. A focus on heroes not immediately connected with the Alamo compound may also allow a transference of favorite symbolic acts away from the Alamo trinity. For example, the physical examination of Milam's skeletal remains has led one scholar to hypothesize that Ben Milam had severe arthritis in his hips, and that he probably used some sort of support for walking, such as a cane. A few accounts of the 1835 Texan attack on San Antonio led by Milam declare that Milam drew a line in the dirt, requiring that men willing to fight with him cross the line. If Milam used a cane, the logic now runs, he could have used it to draw the line in the dirt dividing the faint-hearted from the men willing to give their lives for Texas. People interested in this hypothesis have suggested that Travis may have been credited around campfires for the inspirational act performed by Ben Milam. Apparently, much symbolic "property" is at stake in the study of "old Ben's bones."

A focus on "property" not controlled by the DRT suggests one way in which people dissatisfied with the past currently presented at the Alamo can combat that past. But the most obvious means of expressing anger at the DRT-sponsored history remains organized public protest. The popularity of the Alamo as a protest spot increases along with the rising Hispanic population and political awareness in San Antonio. The experience of *Washington Post* writer James T. Yenckel on his visit to the Alamo is not unusual:

> Across the street from Alamo Plaza, a crowd of perhaps 150 Mexican American scholars—so identified on their name tags— had gathered in an anti-Alamo protest. . . . In speeches, the protest leaders cited the Alamo as the symbol of their anger about what they see is wrong with the country. . . . To them, the Alamo represents what amounted to the Yankee theft of Texas from Mexico and, they contended, Mexican Americans today are still getting a raw deal from a government they see dominated by unsympathetic Anglo-Americans. "White man's history is not enough," read one large banner. With that introduction, I suspect I viewed the display inside the Alamo of Davy Crockett's beaded

buckskin vest with the onyx buttons with somewhat less awe than I might have on my first childhood visit.

(*Washington Post*, June 21, 1992)

The writer's feeling "somewhat less awe" toward the Alamo heroes shows the success of outsiders, the supposedly illegitimate heirs. Any public presentation held "in the street"—be it protest, ceremony, or reenactment—has a newfound legitimacy whereas "the institution" in American society (in this case, the Alamo, the DRT, and the State of Texas) is losing ground as the omniscient authority at American historic sites.

# Chapter 9. Heroes in the Street

People who must remain outside "in the street" to reproduce their versions of the Alamo's past declare that the history at the Alamo, as presented by the Daughters of the Republic of Texas, excludes much of the city's (and the nation's) population from the site's heritage. In this viewpoint, the Alamo, under the DRT's care, cradles primarily Anglo society, most particularly wealthy Anglo society.

However, not all people dissatisfied with the DRT's version of the Alamo's past reject the Alamo as a symbol or the DRT's favorite figures, the Alamo defenders. These more respectful "protestors" view the past presented at the Alamo as simply "sterile," and some feel that the city of San Antonio has a responsibility to rejuvenate the Alamo compound's past. Robert Benavides explained this problem and potential to visitors during his narration of the 1989 Fiesta event This Hallowed Ground, Alamo Plaza:

> Have any of you stood on this side of the street [across from Alamo Plaza] and said, "Oh, look, across the street. There's the Alamo," and you were already standing in the Alamo; you were on hallowed ground. . . . The Alamo compound was more than three acres in size. About 25 percent of the Alamo compound, which includes the chapel, the Long Barracks, and the courtyard area, is owned by the State of Texas. . . . Two-thirds, 60 to 65 percent . . . is owned by the City of San Antonio. When they [San Antonians] were approached with this fact, they suddenly realized that they not only had a majority ownership of a national historic landmark, but a majority of responsibility to change this plaza from something that was historically sterile, relatively speaking, to address the fact that, yes, this is the first of our famous five missions, and it certainly is also the hallowed ground of the Alamo [battle].
>
> (1989 This Hallowed Ground, Alamo Plaza)

The city—San Antonians, the "they" of this perspective—owns over half of the Alamo compound and therefore should have a voice in how the past is presented at the site. This speech, intentionally or not, suggests the city-versus-state division at the Alamo, a distinction which is important since San Antonio's population is predominantly Hispanic whereas the state's population is predominantly Anglo.

This Hallowed Ground, Alamo Plaza, is a tour of the Alamo compound offered annually at Fiesta by the William B. Travis Chapter of the Sons of the Republic of Texas. (The tour is also offered in February on the anniversary of the first day of the Alamo siege, and on March 6.) The tour, presented for the first time as part of the 1986 sesquicentennial celebration of Texas' independence, is now an official Fiesta San Antonio event. Benavides, a past president of this chapter, wrote the script for the tour and serves as its narrator.

The SRT organization, with bloodline requirements similar to those of the DRT, has proportionately more Hispanic members than does the DRT. The organization's stated objectives differ slightly from those of the DRT, with one of the main differences being the historical research encouraged by the SRT. The SRT organization does not place, in its stated objectives concerning historical research, the emphasis on post-1835 Texas history required by the DRT. Thus, the SRT appears more open to research of Hispanic contributions to the site, before and after the 1836 battle.

The first attempt to form the SRT began in 1895, four years after the DRT formed, but the SRT did not come into being until 1922, and was not chartered until 1934. According to one SRT member, the organization has not, until recently, been as active as the DRT. Prior to 1986, the SRT had been primarily a social group, meeting quarterly and having a couple of organized dinners a year. But since the 1986 Texas sesquicentennial, the SRT, in conjunction with the San Antonio Living Historians Association (SALHA), has become more socially and politically active. In that year, the living historians, who are now part of SALHA, participated in the SRT's presentation of This Hallowed Ground.

The 1986 sesquicentennial also served as a beginning of SALHA itself, which formed from the Alamo Lore and Myth organization. In its history pamphlet, SALHA notes that it is a nonprofit organization "dedicated to educating the public about historical events, battles, lifestyles, customs, and cultures that were prevalent in Texas during its struggle for independence, circa 1830's." SALHA members are reenactors who "are developing first-person identities and maintaining them throughout the events" sponsored by SALHA

(1989 SALHA pamphlet). Via these identities, SALHA members create kinship ties with the battle imagery of the Alamo similar to such kinship created by the Texas Cavaliers.

In their presentations about the Alamo's past, the SRT and SALHA have attempted to enliven the history for the entire, three-acre compound. The SRT and SALHA members strive to instill in their audience an awe of the battle and of the heroes they impersonate. One of the ways in which they enliven history at the Alamo is to warn the audience of impending danger as they make the past present, especially when they reenact the 1836 battle. During the 1990 Victory or Death program, the narrator prepared the audience for the danger to come:

> Narrator: As soon as we get the Mexican soldiers into position, they're going to have to take a position up on the curb. If you would allow them to take a position there, please, before they go into a battle stance . . . just kind of back aside; otherwise they're liable to lance you. Secondly, the cannon crew has asked that we make a special announcement for you. The cannon that is going off today is a four-pounder mountain howitzer; it looks like a small one but it lets off with a loud bang. . . . When the cannon goes off, the position for you to be in is probably with your ears closed. . . . Also if you would just leave your mouth slightly ajar. . . . Also we ask that no one proceed in front of the cannon as soon as the program begins. Do not cut across the street in front of that; we do not want to have an accident with someone thinking it's just a blank charge. A blank charge from a twelve pound howitzer can still take your head off.
>
> (1990 Victory or Death)

The audience must feel the foretold doom that the presence of the soldiers brings to the site, as well as the danger these reenactors control, making authentic the visitors' experience.

All visitors surviving the reenacted march of the Mexican soldiers and the cannon blast were later invited to enter into the spirit of the reenactment by crossing Travis's line in the dirt redrawn by the Living Historians. Once the civilian troops had been prepared during the 1990 ceremony, the SALHA member portraying Travis offered the following requirements of those who would cross the line:

> Travis reenactor: Ladies and gentlemen, the line I have drawn is symbolic for the line, whether it's symbolic, legend, or fact, that

confronts and challenges us even to this day, even in this country. Each of you must decide what form of freedom this line means to you, and when you cross that line you must realize, are you prepared to die for what you believe in as these men one hundred and fifty-four years ago did. Blood was spilled here in the name of liberty, ladies and gentlemen. Please tread softly. Those of you who would choose to make the same decision as the men of the Alamo, cross that line [drum roll].

(1990 Victory or Death)

The reenactors work to pull the audience/tourists into their version of the past; through the audience participation, the reenactors validate their ties to the site and their right to be the descendants of the heroes in appearance, spirit, and action. They are living history—visible, audible, and tangible. After the program is over, they are there for any questions the audience may have, and they invite those questions; they strive to be the historical authority on the site.

The drawing of Travis's line adds the familiar, but this line is more than familiarity. It forms a boundary as much as the DRT's version of Travis's line. The DRT's version is a brass line which, in 1989, the organization had placed in the stone walk directly in front of the Alamo's front doors. An accompanying brass plaque reads:

Legend states that in 1836 Lt. Col. William Barret Travis unsheathed his sword and drew a line on this ground before his battle weary men, stating, "Those prepared to give their lives in freedom's cause come over to me."

Those who would cross the line supposedly do so in the mind-set of those who draw it. Both versions of Travis's line declare a popular part of the creation myth to be valid in understanding what the Alamo is, and both require commitment on the part of those who cross them.

With the different lines comes competition for which is more authentic. One Living Historian claimed the line SALHA drew as the more authentic, for their Travis drew it within city property on what would have been near the center of the compound. However, it lacks the permanence of the DRT-sponsored line, at least visually.

The different lines reveal the perceived importance of claiming the past. Intimate ties to the past give authority and control, and the Living Historians, not being the state-sanctioned presenters of the past, must court connections whenever possible. In a move creating this authority, some SALHA members donned their period dress when archaeologists were working in 1988 on the area where the compound's south wall stood; and the SALHA members served as informants to tourists curious about the excavation (*Austin American-Statesman*, July 7, 1988). The Living Historians held artifacts unearthed in the project for tourists to view. In their appearance and in the objects they held, the Living Historians strove to present a past more real and involving to tourists than that offered by the DRT.

The past presented by the SRT and SALHA contains inheritance claims beyond artifacts, for the Living Historians assume the identity of people involved in the 1836 battle, thereby giving these heroes a first-person presence. These reenactors both form and are formed by the characters they portray during the reenactments. A man and a woman who had never met before were cast as husband and wife, Almeron and Susanna Dickinson, for one of the reenactments; they married after this "fateful" casting, and consider March 6, the anniversary of the heroes' deaths, their anniversary. They see themselves as continuing in the present the heroes of the past, taking up where they left off. This casting has become a permanent part of who they are, and they continue their annual pilgrimage to the birth site of their new lives.

This couple's new lives from the heroes' deaths echoes the regenerative theme of the Texas creation mythology. But their receiving identity on March 6 actually runs counter to the SALHA's official stance toward this most sacred day for the reenactors. For the March 6 ceremony, associations with particular heroes supposedly dissolve. Though there are no set roles in this ceremony, it has the air of reenactment with a collapsing of time and a proclaimed immediacy. The announcer of the 1990 Dawn at the Alamo declared that at the time the ceremony begins, "hundreds of people [stand] in their own silent vigil." The event of the past is brought to the present in a sacred repetition, much as the Christian Stations of the Cross on Good Friday meditatively retraces Christ's last steps.

In the 1990 Dawn at the Alamo presentation, a narrator recounted the events that occurred "here" and "on this morning"; the time of death was announced and observed. At this point in the presentation, a chaplain offered a prayer in which he commemorated the dead Texans, but he also called for a commemoration of the Mexican dead. He closed with a verbal swipe that could have been aimed at critics of the heroes, such as Jeff Long, and/or at the DRT for their criticism of the honoring of Mexican dead:

We stand here, oh Lord, on this morning at the hour of their sacrifice to humbly remember the men of the Alamo who represent
twenty-one states and seven countries. . . . We also stand, oh
Lord, here to pay lasting tribute to the brave *soldados* . . . who
fought here for the honor of their republic and whose blood was
spilled here without discretion. . . . We ask, oh Heavenly Father,
that in this busy world that the memories of such brave people
will always be maintained and that we, despite the critics and
the cynics, will always have the courage and honor to remember
them.

(1990 Dawn at the Alamo)

Whoever the target, the parting shot defended the SRT and SALHA
focus within the ceremony; it also prepared the audience for the gun
salute to the Mexican army later in the ceremony.

The two types of performances at the Alamo—reenactment and
commemorative ceremony—are the means by which the SRT and
SALHA establish their connection to the site in their own eyes
and in the eyes of the public. To prove their understanding of the
site's importance to the public, the SRT and SALHA members offer
a reverent and familiar past. Their reverence reflects their appropriate attitude toward the site, and their warnings of danger in weaponry add surprise as well as an appeal to authenticity to their
performance.

This authenticity as experienced in the blank charges from the
reenactors' cannon has drawn complaints from the DRT members.
Some DRT members feel that the cannon blasts are disruptive, if not
to the buildings themselves, then at least to the aura within them.
(I have not heard similar complaints about the Texas Cavaliers' use
of cannon fire within the compound to welcome the new King Antonio.) Some of the DRT members further disparage the reenactments themselves; one member depicted the SRT and SALHA members as playing cops and robbers out on the plaza.

Similarly, some SRT and SALHA members have expressed dissat-
isfaction with the DRT and its control of the site. However, in con-
tradiction to appearances (or for the sake of appearances), relations
between the DRT and these two outsider groups are improving; one
SRT member noted, as proof of this improvement, that they had
been asked to participate in the DRT's March 2 ceremony held outside Alamo Hall.

Despite the occasional friction, few within the SRT and SALHA
wish to see the DRT supplanted as custodian. The Living Historians

are particularly concerned about who would be custodian in the DRT's stead. One reenactor expressed concern at the suggestion that Texas Parks and Wildlife serve as custodian, claiming that this state agency would be mostly interested in the mission period rather than in the 1836 battle. This reenactor knows that if the mission period is stressed, his connection to the site (portraying Alamo combatants) disappears, or is at least demoted in importance. Logically enough, reenactors are interested almost entirely in the 1836 battle, for it is that event and period with which they have created their identity. This interest places reenactors more in the DRT's camp than in that of people wishing to illuminate the Alamo's mission heritage.

Furthermore, the battle imagery is what sells both in the shops and theaters surrounding the plaza and within the DRT gift shop/ museum. Mission life as presented in textbooks and popular history texts does not usually offer the drama given war. Anyone wishing to create a public identity with this site must ideologically cross over Travis's line and become in league with the Alamo heroes, a move that may be especially difficult for Hispanics.

Still, the programs in which the SRT and SALHA work together attempt to address both interests (i.e., battle and mission). Of their joint ventures, the presentation offering the most mission period history is the walking tour written by Robert Benavides: This Hallowed Ground, Alamo Plaza; its script reveals a particularly strong attempt to integrate mission and battle imagery and to declare the Hispanic ancestry of the site and some of its heroes. The speech offered by the reenactor portraying Juan Abamillo notes the number of Tejano defenders and the area they had been given to defend. But in the description of the area defended by the Tejanos, mission period history is interjected, defining the area as the gate through which Indians and mission clergy passed during the mission period of the compound.

In this speech, the battle aura is interrupted by mission history so that the Tejano defender, in this case portrayed by a Hispanic man, can declare the Hispanic claim to the site prior to the battle. That claim is reinforced later in this speech by the words awarded one of the Tejano defenders, Toribio Losoya, who declares that he was born in the compound and he will die there (1989 This Hallowed Ground, Alamo Plaza).

In this scenario, the Hispanic male is the original child of the Alamo; in the minds of some Hispanics in San Antonio, he has been unjustly displaced by the Anglo female: Angelina Dickinson in the mythology, and the DRT in society. As this is the first speech by a reenactor during the tour, the Tejano defenders' role is the first impression the audience receives about the battle; in this version of the Alamo battle, the Tejanos are first in San Antonio and within the Alamo itself.

Other Hispanic male contributions to the site, especially those made prior to the 1836 battle, surface throughout the Hallowed Ground tour via descriptions offered by the narrator. At one point he notes the Hispanic man from whom the Alamo received its name: San Carlos de Parras del Alamo. This focus on a Hispanic man as the namesake of the Alamo contrasts with the DRT's favored origin of "Alamo" as meaning cottonwood tree, which is a "natural" part of the site. In the written history offered to schoolteachers visiting the Alamo, the DRT presents both possible origins of the Alamo name. But on an individual basis, informants (such as the tour guide for a fourth-grade class and a member of the Alamo Chapter) usually give "cottonwood" as the favored origin. In contrast, the version offered by the walking tour has a Hispanic man as the unquestioned source of the famous Alamo name.

Furthermore, one portion of the Hallowed Ground tour suggests that the Alamo compound contains more Spanish and Indian blood than blood of the Alamo defenders. In the script the narrator declares that the burials performed on the site during the mission period initially hallowed the site with the interment of more than a thousand Christianized Indians, Spanish soldiers, and civilians (1989 This Hallowed Ground, Alamo Plaza). The implication is that Hispanics first hallowed the site, and with more bodies.

Focus on Hispanics at the site rubs some DRT members the wrong way, especially when the Hispanics presented as admirable are part of the Mexican army. These relatively nameless historic figures, who serve as executioners in the Texas creation mythology, are the ultimate outsiders. Perhaps that is why Robert Benavides gives them a sympathetic role in the walking-tour script. The Mexican *soldado*'s speech explains that Santa Anna marched the Mexican army eight hundred miles to fight in Texas with the intent of putting down a rebellion instigated by the United States. In this narrative, the Mexican is rightly the one on the administrative inside, a control that has been unjustly taken from him.

But the division between the inside and the outside at the Alamo becomes a slippery one, especially in reenactments: Are the Hispanics, by their declared ethnicity, on the inside of the Alamo among the missionaries and the Tejano defenders, or are they on the outside as Mexicans? This duality appeared during the 1989 Hallowed Ground program in the reenactor who portrayed the 1836 Mexican *soldado*. When it was his turn to speak, he was razzed by the audience, but still offered the less popular view of the Texans as rebels rather than revolutionists. He then cried, "¡Viva Santa Anna!" and engaged one of the "defenders" in a combative pose. But at the end of the tour this Mexican soldier changed sides and joined in the salute to the Alamo defenders (Fig. 9.1).[1]

Perhaps the reenactors simply needed more bodies and/or men who knew how to fire one of the reproduction rifles for the salute. But intentionally or not, the figure portrays the inside/outside dichotomy facing Hispanics wishing to claim the popularized past at the Alamo. In this past, Hispanics must drop their Mexican identity and ideologically cross Travis's line, stretching as the border between Mexico and Texas; they must fall in with the men fighting to transform Tejas into Texas.

Benavides's involvement with Alamo Plaza exemplifies this split. He is reverent to the memory of proclaimed heroes, such as Milam and the Alamo defenders, who fought to separate Texas from Mexico. But the script he wrote and copyrighted, This Hallowed Ground, Alamo Plaza, gives voice to strong Hispanic claims to the site, both before and after the 1836 battle, and inside and outside the walls of the battle arena. The script attempts to re-create Hispanic accomplishments—missionary and military—muted during the past 150 years.

Benavides's script gives claim to the site via Hispanic males, but Benavides is also part of a move to recognize the work of Adina De Zavala at the site via a plaque on city property. Although some DRT members have purportedly suggested that the plaque should be placed at De Zavala's grave site, the group pressing for the plaque on Alamo Plaza wants the high visibility that the plaza offers. De Zavala's image has been successfully subordinated to Clara Driscoll's in the Alamo museums, but now this Hispanic woman, held outside this property during the last years of her life, is being declared insider once again by those outside.

The associations and feelings between individuals and groups—who is inside, who outside—are complex, even within the SRT and SALHA groups. The tension I describe between the DRT, the SRT, and SALHA is what I perceive in talking with members of the various groups. When asked point-blank, most members of these groups will deny that there is tension between or within them. But comments offered "off the record" (i.e., when the informant turned off the tape recorder or when the comments came in an unguarded moment) suggest that ethnically defined tensions exist within the groups and between them. My personal opinion is that the Anglo-versus-Hispanic issues are silent sore spots, especially within the

Fig. 9.1. Battle Reenactment.

SALHA organization. Though both appear as outsiders in relation to the state-appointed custodians, the DRT, there is not a feeling of total harmony between the SRT and SALHA. When one of the SALHA members expressed an interest in seeing someone of their "caliber" taking over the history of the site, I wondered about the potential for division within the groups if the DRT were to lose control of the site, and if the SRT and SALHA were to gain any influence in how the site is administered. My impression is that some members would push for emphasis on Hispanic contributions to the site, and others would want to focus almost solely on the heroic acts of the Alamo defenders.

What brings the SRT and SALHA together—as well as other outsider groups—is a feeling of exclusion and the desire for association with the Alamo compound. Union is easily declared, by both outsiders and insiders. What rumbles underground is the tension within. Probing this tension reveals the energy source of identity at the site, for identity is formed less by "common characteristics" than by undeclared differences.

# Chapter 10. Analysts

The tensions between and within groups controlling the Alamo's past and those who would control it create, for scholars researching the site, intriguing yet frustrating barriers. This is especially true for anthropologists who depend on people for their social analysis. Fear (often undefinable) silences informants, some refusing to talk and others reaching over and turning off the tape recorder. Even though most informants enjoy describing the current social conflicts at the Alamo, few are willing to have these battles committed to the printed page, at least not in a traceable manner.

However, the vast majority of researchers focusing on the Alamo—historians and archaeologists—do not have to face this particular barrier because their research does not depend heavily on living informants. For these scholars, one of the stumbling blocks has been, at least in the past, the Daughters' overriding emphasis on the 1836 battle. Many DRT members typify historical preservers whose main explicit objective is to keep the past as presented from being "lost" or altered. For the DRT, the relevant history at the Alamo begins with the 1836 battle.

This emphasis on the past from 1836 onward is hardly surprising; the DRT identity springs from the birth of Texas as an independent republic at the Alamo, "the cradle of Texas liberty." In a focus on the mission period, the vast majority of DRT members, as the group is currently defined, would have no ancestral identity, and therefore they have little interest, as a group, in forwarding research of that period. Archaeologist Anne Fox described the resistance she experienced initially at the DRT Library when trying to research the mission period of the site:

> Twenty years ago no one in the DRT library was encouraged to research anything about the Alamo prior to the 1836 battle. They [the DRT] tended to blot out that whole period of history. . . . So

of course we immediately got in trouble with them because our interest was even more in the mission period, archaeologically.

(Fox 1990)

Fox explained that the attitude at the library has changed, with more mission period studies being accepted.

Fox's colleague Waynne Cox explained that the DRT are indeed allowing more focus on the mission period, but that this change is a matter not of choice but of necessity:

To some extent, they're yielding—rather reluctantly, because, of course, their interest is "13 days" [the 1836 siege] exclusively. . . . They're trying to appease the Mexican-American side that was harassing them.

(Cox 1990)

Cox felt that the DRT was giving "lip service" to the Hispanic community's demands for more interest in the past at the Alamo because of the growing political strength of Hispanics, but that the DRT's recognition of Hispanic contributions to the site is given begrudgingly. In the eyes of the DRT members the "13 days to glory" still provide the primary importance of the site (Cox 1990). To give equal emphasis to the mission period or to honor the Mexican soldiers who fought in the battle is to empower an identity created by other groups within San Antonio.

But the DRT's focus on the 1836 battle is only a minor barrier for researchers; the major one is the DRT's management. Fox claimed that the DRT are currently difficult to deal with because their system is "terribly inefficient": "They have a complete turnover in officers every year, and there's hardly ever any continuity to speak of. You never know who you are dealing with. Things change overnight; suddenly everything is different" (Fox 1990). What Fox did not note, however, is that such "inefficiency" serves as a very effective buffer between the DRT and those who would criticize decisions made by their governing body, the Alamo Committee. Blame is difficult to place with such rapid turnover in command.

But even when the head officer of the Alamo Committee *does* commit herself on paper, other DRT members may deny that she represents the organization. Such denial surfaced in the 1994 controversy surrounding the city's attempt to close the street in front of the Alamo church. A journalist covering the story, David McLemore, noted that in 1986 the chairwoman of the Alamo Committee, Edith Mae Johnson, sent a statement on the DRT stationery urging that the city close this street. But the 1994 chairwoman, Anna Hartman, claimed that Johnson's action—even though performed as the 1986 chairwoman of the Alamo Committee—was not "official" and represented Johnson's opinion rather than that of the DRT organization (*Dallas Morning News*, March 5, 1994). For researchers attempting to understand the organization's official stance on issues involving the Alamo, the DRT members sometimes appear unwilling to accept responsibility for the actions of their officers, even when performed in a *seemingly* official capacity.

Anne Fox also finds the DRT's apprehensiveness toward researchers troublesome; the DRT is very sensitive to any criticism of any sort. But if Fox is critical of the DRT's stance in relation to the Alamo, she is also critical of some of the Hispanics who use the DRT and the Alamo as a target for their protests. She depicts the more vocal protesters as people "who have reason to keep this [the animosity between early Texans and Mexicans] alive," and declared that researchers have to discount that faction as well (Fox 1990).

The social and political pressures surrounding the Alamo complicate for Fox and other archaeologists the dilemma of what the past means within the present, and what role the archaeologist has in defining the past of this site. The Alamo offers a particularly sensitive scenario for the archaeologist wishing to bring artifacts to the light of day, for a focus on the mission period requires going outside the boundary of state-owned property to include the outer, predominantly city-owned part of the Alamo mission compound. When archaeologists seek the foundations of the various walls, they define boundaries which, in the current power struggle on Alamo Plaza, better serve the Hispanic crusade than the DRT's focus. Some of the politically active Hispanics both encourage and are encouraged by the archaeological research on the mission period of the Alamo, which necessarily stresses Hispanic origins within Texas and the city's majority ownership of the "hallowed ground."

But archaeologists forming their interpretations of the Alamo (and other historic sites) face still another pressure: tourists' expectations. No matter what their focus may be for excavations on Alamo Plaza (mission period or 1836 battle), the comments from Anne Fox and her co-workers regarding the excavations must please, to some extent, the public; the Alamo still attracts visitors primarily because of the 1836 battle. The excavations themselves are popular news items when they are in progress, and the physical settings become part of the tourist attractions at the Alamo. During the 1988 excavation on the south wall, an Austin newspaper reporter claimed that the excavation "seemed to be drawing as much reverent attention from the tourists as the indoor exhibits on David Crockett, William Travis and the other heroes of 1836" (*Austin American-Statesman*, July 7, 1988).

Even when Fox and the other UTSA archaeologists are focusing primarily on the mission period structures and artifacts during an excavation, the publicity for the research often focuses on the possibility of more sensational discoveries associated with the 1836 battle. A good example of twisted purpose statements occurred during the 1984 excavation. (The excavation was made possible because of clearing an area near Alamo Plaza to build a new shopping mall.) Although Anne Fox and Waynne Cox were primarily looking for structural foundations and artifacts of the mission period, a reporter from Houston downplayed their primary interest of learning more about how the Spanish friars developed the mission as a means of settling Texas. He gave his article a headline focused instead on Fox's comment that the most sensational discovery would be the charred bones of the cremated Alamo defenders: "UT Scientists Hope to Uncover Funeral Pyre of Alamo Heroes." The reporter depicts Fox and Cox as "racing an urban developer's bulldozers in a long-shot bid to uncover one of the saddest monuments in American history" (*Houston Chronicle*, November 25, 1984).

But the interchange between the archaeologists' interests and tourists' expectations is more dialectical than it may seem; some archaeologists have played upon the public's interest in the site to create more interest in their discoveries. The different ways in which individual archaeologists have responded to the publicity at this site are reflected in the following passages from two reports on different excavations on Alamo Plaza:

[From *The Stratigraphy, Features and Artifacts*, 1967 excavation]

The period of the seige [*sic*] of 1836 seems to be primarily represented by a small feature in the north courtyard. This was a concentration of early Anglo-American material on the inside edge of what appears to have been the north wall of the Alamo property during the time of the seige [*sic*], and just inside the present north wall. The material included large amounts of white-paste earthenware . . . , gun flints, gun parts, musket, rifle, and pistol balls, part of a bugle and other items apparently dating to this period and left during the battle.

(Greer 1967:100–101)

[From *Excavations at the Alamo Shrine*, 1980 excavation]

At the time of the 1836 battle, most of the mission buildings were still standing, although in sad need of repairs; and they were used as refuge by those 182 men who drew the line and kept their place to await destiny.

The Mexican artillery commander was ordered to immediately set up his two 8-inch howitzers and to fire four grenades (spherical case) into the Alamo. Fragments of spherical shells were found during the archaeological excavations. The exploding shell, although doing little actual damage, had definite impact on the defenders.

(Eaton 1980: 1, 9)


The simple listing of battle artifacts by John Greer contrasts sharply with Jack Eaton's attempt to pull his reader into the past with his dramatic description of the site at the time of the 1836 battle and the archaeological data retrieved from the excavation. Eaton wants his reader to feel an emotional tie with the past as researched and "recovered."

The tone Eaton employs may result from what Anne Fox calls the biggest barrier facing archaeology at the Alamo: funding. The excavations in 1989 and 1990 were funded indirectly by money from a private source interested in "interpretation" on Alamo Plaza; the original designs for this interpretation were canceled, and the money was allotted for archaeological research instead. Although Fox claims that the funds were not originally set aside to further the battle imagery at the site, the proposed use had included an eternal flame to be dedicated to the Alamo heroes (Fox 1990). This "interpretation," in conjunction with the cenotaph on Alamo Plaza, would have made concrete the sacrifice imagery of the site. Archaeology is also expected to supply concrete evidence of the past—preferably the 1836 past, in this ideology.

Although the archaeologists conducting research on the Alamo grounds feel the pressures to satisfy popular images and avoid political clashes, few of the researchers feel this pressure as much as the executive director of the Texas Historical Commission (THC), Curtis Tunnell. Tunnell was the first state archaeologist for Texas, a position created in 1965, initially under the State Building Commission. Evolving through the Texas Historical Survey and the State Antiquities Committee, the Texas Historical Commission was formed in the early 1970s. As the current executive director, Tunnell is the one to whom the DRT reports, supposedly, before "driving a nail" at the Alamo. But as Tunnell explained, the DRT's authority at the site is undefined:

> It is unclear in their [the DRT members'] minds, and it's certainly unclear to us [the Texas Historical Commission] where the lines are drawn, what they can do at their discretion and what they need to coordinate with the governor's office. I think there isn't real clear responsibility in a lot of ways at that site. And being our premier historic property in the state of Texas, it's unfortunate that there is ambiguity as to who does what and so forth. . . . That site is so important that there really should be—and someday I hope there will be—real careful control and management. It should be professionally, *very* professionally managed. . . . However the Alamo is managed, it should be one of our best-managed properties.
>
> (Tunnell 1990)

Tunnell acknowledged only a limited control over how the DRT presents the past at the Alamo. For example, the DRT has taken as its prerogative the placement and removal of plaques declaring historic importance. Tunnell claimed not to have been consulted on Travis's line being placed in stone with the accompanying plaque; nor was he told initially of the DRT's plan to replace several 1922 brass plaques containing historical vignettes with plaques containing revised vignettes. He heard of the removal indirectly, and learned that the DRT had intended to melt down the old plaques. He managed to view the 1922 plaques and requested that they be curated rather than destroyed (Tunnell 1990). Although the DRT contacts Tunnell for physical changes that involve the structural integrity of the buildings, such as pointing the walls of the church, the presentation of the past they take into their own hands.

Nor does the Texas Historical Commission control which past is presented at this state historic property. Tunnell commented that as an archaeologist his main interest is the mission period of the site, but this is not what DRT members choose to emphasize; they see the site as a *shrine* to the Alamo defenders, a designation the DRT has awarded the site and to which, Tunnell explained, the members are very attached.

Tunnell and others within the THC balance their criticisms and concern for the DRT's management of the Alamo with praise for the organization's accomplishments. Tunnell's speech during the 1990 March 6 memorial service performed such a balancing act: He risked the ire of the DRT in recommending that all soldiers fighting during the 1836 battle (including the Mexican soldiers) be recognized and honored for their valor (suggesting that such a recognition is not a part of the DRT's presentation of the past), but he ended the speech with praise for the DRT's pointing of the church walls. Similarly, during my interview with him, Tunnell implied that there are definite problems in the way in which the DRT members manage the Alamo, but he ended by saying, "There were years when they [the DRT members] were the only ones who cared enough to try to do something [with the Alamo grounds]" (Tunnell 1990).

Tunnell, in balancing criticism with praise, acknowledges the work that the DRT organization has done in maintaining the state-owned part of the Alamo compound. But such balancing may also be a politically wise stance. The THC is a relatively young and small agency within the state government, having only sixty-five employees; as such it has little political clout in comparison to the larger and more politically powerful DRT. Accordingly, THC members must be careful in their dealings with DRT members and in things said about them. Even larger organizations back away from the DRT. According to a THC employee, Texas Parks and Wildlife, a department which has been considered for replacing the DRT as custodians of the Alamo, "won't touch the issue of management with a ten-foot pole" (THC member 1989).

Another state agency which handles the DRT with care is the Texas Education Agency, as revealed in a 1992 encounter between the DRT and state education officials. The meeting between the groups concerned a proposal to change fourth-grade social studies from a primarily Texas studies course to one with a broader, international focus. (Not at question was seventh-grade Texas history, which focuses on Texas' development.) A reporter for the *Houston Post* described the exchange:

In the latest battle of the Alamo, the Daughters of the Republic of Texas drew a line for protecting Texas history in the fourth grade and state education officials quietly retreated. The June 24 showdown in a hall on the Alamo grounds in San Antonio pitted more than 50 Texana devotees against a proposal giving traditional fourth-grade Social Studies an international, multicultural flavor.

(*Houston Post*, July 7, 1992)

The DRT appears here as undefeatable, drawing the line once again at the Alamo and forcing those in opposition to retreat in silence.

The concern over the political and social power of the DRT and the other groups intimately associated with the Alamo affects those with something to lose (i.e., jobs, customers, or image). And such concern hampers, to an extent, fieldwork for anthropologists as well as archaeologists. During my interviews with Hispanic community leaders, some of the informants would either reach over and turn off the tape recorder or motion for me to turn it off so that they could feel free to express anger toward groups and imagery associated with the Alamo. Although none of my Anglo informants required the same action, some were exceedingly careful about what they said. One DRT member with whom I spoke was very concerned over what would be done with the interview material, saying that she did not want to be identified by name; in the end, she decided not even to be quoted.

I now understand the balancing act archaeologists have performed at the Alamo since the 1960s, an act anthropologists will have to perform as well if we hope to continue researching the site. The DRT receives all scholars—anyone asking questions—cautiously *if* at all. The silence of informants is a major threat to anthropological research.

But this silence is information itself, for it highlights sensitive arenas. When Jeff Long published *Duel of Eagles*, he made a serious effort to thank as many people associated with the DRT and its library as possible, and then he eagerly awaited the DRT's response—in vain. The DRT preferred to remain silent rather than give this dissident the satisfaction of hearing its members seethe publicly. Instead, the members focused their anger inside for their own uses. I received from a DRT member a taped copy of radio personality Alan Dale's interview with Jeff Long; she had as her mission the dispersal of these tapes, which she felt revealed Long's ineptitude. A feeling expressed by some DRT members is that Long, having only been born in Texas but raised in Colorado, is not a "real" Texan. "Real" Texans can be trusted with Texas history and will handle it properly.

A silent response to Jeff Long revealed the dislike and distrust the DRT felt toward this pseudo-Texan. But even born-and-reared Texans are rejected if they don't offer the type of "history" espoused by George McAlister, who has been well received by the DRT. Despite my having been born in San Antonio, raised in Paris, Texas, and educated at the University of Texas, the DRT members who spoke with me remained cautious, trying to determine if I could be trusted.

The DRT members with whom I spoke certainly did not offer all information freely, especially in reference to the Order of the Alamo's and the Texas Cavaliers' private use of the Alamo church. These privileges are definitely not advertised by the DRT, for even Curtis Tunnell of the THC seemed surprised upon hearing of this special use of Texas' premier historic property. One DRT member explained that these privileges were granted because the Order of the Alamo and the Texas Cavaliers had been using the site for some time. Such reasoning implies that these groups have been granted the right to use the Alamo by the hand of tradition, and so are exempt from the need to seek approval elsewhere.

In addition to the silent stance the DRT and others can assume, researchers such as Michaele Haynes, Anne Fox, and Waynne Cox have the added difficulty of living in the same city of their research. The strain is less for one who studies the region and then leaves. But even for those living outside of Texas, the sociopolitical tensions are real enough when working in the midst of them. During the protest staged by the Revolutionary Communist Youth Brigade in 1991, I was approached after the demonstration by a man who appeared to be Hispanic and who had been watching me photograph and record the protestors. After we had introduced ourselves, he asked me how I "felt" about the protest. I explained that I didn't *feel* anything, that I was studying how people used the Alamo. He became angry and said that the problem with "scientists," such as me, was that we didn't feel, that we had no emotions. He declared his affiliation with the protestors and their group, and then pressed to know where I was staying.

But in all honesty, I had felt something upon hearing the protestors refer to the Alamo as the beginning of the American Southwest. My analysis supports the depiction of the Alamo "history" as a creation myth for Texas as well as the rest of the American Southwest. Upon hearing this same sentiment from the mouths of such extremists, I began to feel a fear for how my research would be used; I began to feel the awkward responsibilities of a "repatriated anthropologist," as described by Richard Handler:

[P]erhaps what is most intriguing about a repatriated anthropology is that the normally empathetic relationship with "their people" that anthropologists cultivate . . . may "at home" give way to a kind of dialogic participation that does not exclude dis-

agreement and mutual criticism. . . . [T]he insider-outsider distinction has power and relevance, and the anthropologist-as-
insider may feel freer to transform cultural analysis into cultural
criticism as anthropological discourse enters into and engages
the discourse of society at large. As participants and observers at
home, it is both a responsibility and a privilege for anthropologists to develop informed criticisms to be debated and shared
among their people.

(Handler 1988:2)

Criticism I can offer—and feel I should offer—extends to *all* who
use the Alamo for declaring identity, especially to the end of sup-
pressing or manipulating others. In the process of analyzing this
site, I have exchanged my own identity—that of liberal Texan—for
that of anthropologist.

# Conclusion. The Responsible Anthropologist

The suggestion by Richard Handler that anthropologists serve as social critics of their own society suits well the tenor of anthropology. Our field is notorious for attracting individuals who feel alienated in one way or another from society: we go seeking alternatives. Whether visiting another society or studying our own, we often enter our studies with some notion of what we think a society *should* be, and with a bone to pick with our own. Roy Wagner claims that the "evangelistic message" of anthropology is one of emancipation: "it draws people who want to emancipate themselves from their culture" (Wagner 1975:10).

Surely some of us use anthropology for personal crusades. In this sense anthropologists are similar to social critics in many other fields (e.g., political science, literary criticism, rhetorical analysis, and social psychology). But, in defense of the social criticism we can offer, the fieldwork done by anthropologists requires an intimacy unknown to archival research and literary analysis. Unexpected sympathies and alienation push against the anthropologist's previous understandings. Interviews with individuals replace, in the mind of the anthropologist, preconceptions about people. Expected paradigms disintegrate, especially when members of the same group deny what each other has said.

This internal disagreement, when presented in the ethnography, denies the social holism previously awarded "culture." Gone is the sense of a unified reality, and in its place is a vocal cacophony. We must let the discord remain if our social analysis and criticism are to have any strength; within this dissonance is the potential for destroying stereotypes both within ourselves and within our informants.

Presenting a discordant society poses a particularly difficult problem for the native anthropologist. We write both to our own and about our own; in writing to our own, we begin a dialogue about ourselves, asking for response to our analysis that will allow us to rethink our presumptions. One of the most sensitive areas of analysis to offer our audience is "the past" as presented. In these ideological blueprints, chaotic events take on a cause-and-effect relationship that orders them and allows people to accept those events and their presumed consequences as logical and necessary. In critical mode, anthropologists question the effect these narratives have on various groups and individuals; we watch the playing out of categories within narratives of the past and are critical of the logic within them. We analyze the past by removing necessity and questioning "truth."

The issue is not the factuality of these narratives but the ordering of the past, the social categories as defined (both implicitly and explicitly), and the conclusions reached. Our job as native anthropologists is to analyze these elements for the "meaning" of the narratives. Our primary role in relation to history is to examine what history (that is, the presentation of the past in narratives, reenactments, and museum exhibits) means to those projecting it and how such history is used; we should not be trying to determine what happened, but rather we should be listening to and analyzing what people *say* happened. These narratives present a unified description of "culture" in their creation of order from chaos, with performances and exhibits sifting people, artifacts, and actions into hierarchical categories. These categories reflect and reinforce the current stereotypes. Anthropologists who study museums and historic sites should work to disassemble that order to the chaos—the vocal cacophony—from which it springs.

One main question arises in the type of analysis presented here: Do anthropologists, in focusing on points of tension and making them explicit in their analysis, make the tensions more real? In my own work, I question whether or not in focusing on the division within the declared unity in San Antonio I have helped fortify differences. In all honesty, I do not believe that I have intensified these boundaries of identity; the lines have been firmly drawn for some time. The Alamo legendry is so powerful and violent that groups wishing to inscribe their names on this site approach it armed with their ethnicity, ready to stereotype the other to gain ground for their own.

One Black female writer brings the Emily West [Morgan] figure into this social battle. Anita Bunkley gives Emily a past in which she is raped by Anglo and Hispanic men, thus villainizing both of those groups. In her preface, Bunkley gives the historic base of her novel:

There were approximately one hundred fifty free Negroes living in the Mexican Province of Tejas during the time of the Battle for Independence in the mid-1830s. Most left little record of their time spent in the frontier, fading silently into the history of the society they helped build. But one of them, Emily D. West, did leave a sketchy trail of her existence. . . . This tapestry of historical figures and fictional characters creates the legend of Emily, the Yellow Rose.

(Bunkley 1989:preface)

One of the review comments printed on the first page of Bunkley's book declares, " 'From a scrap of history, Anita Bunkley has created an absorbing novel,' Sally Dooley, Editor, *Texas Review of Books*." The opposing ethnic groups use these scraps, all equally glad that history is sketchy. One of my informants affiliated with the DRT found comfort in the view of noted historian T. R. Fehrenbach that the Texas Revolution was "a peculiarly undocumented era." This historical haze obscures figures and events, allowing the presenters of the past to make them over in their own image.

Another ethnic claiming of the past comes in Natalie Ornish's study *Pioneer Jewish Texans: Their Impact on Texas and American History for Four Hundred Years, 1590–1990*. In her section on the Texas Revolution, Ornish lists the Jewish Alamo defenders, *including* Louis (Moses) Rose. Ornish feels that Rose "was more like the messenger to Job who said, 'I only am escaped alone to tell thee' " (Ornish 1991:36). Not many groups claim the mythically outcast Rose, but perhaps his image as social pariah makes him an important figure for the Jewish people. One of my colleagues suggested that perhaps Rose, because he was a Jew, was encouraged to leave the Alamo; the others did not want him there.[1]

Unfortunately, when groups attempt to lay claim to this site via ethnically defined figures and when they speculate as to how these figures were treated, the stereotypes and the "logic" of the current San Antonio society—Anglos as dominant, Blacks as oppressed, Jews as rejected, Hispanics as alien—often become amplified rather than corrected. The lines between groups become even more firmly drawn.

The Texas creation mythology is but one example of bounding identity in presentations of the past. All groups have the ability to create such boundaries, as is evident in the work of Ornish and Bunkley. Usually, however, such bounding is done by the dominant group, regardless of that group's declared ethnicity, to protect their dominant status. Anthropologist Ronald Grimes examined such identity divisions in rituals held in Sante Fe, New Mexico, where Hispanic community leaders create public dramas celebrating the 1692 reconquest of the Pueblos by the Spanish force under Don Diego de Vargas. In these public dramas, Hispanics receive the dominant, victorious roles, and native Americans receive the less desirable ones. When the local Indians were unwilling to play their assigned roles in the 1973 De Vargas Entrada pageant, most of the Indian roles for that pageant were played by Hispanic children, many of whom were related to the Caballeros de Vargas, the group sponsoring the pageant. Grimes notes that although a few of the Caballeros later recognized that the casting of children as Indians was problematic and unfortunate, the pageant as performed still supported the image of the Indian as a "childlike primitive" (Grimes 1976:170–171).[2]

One of the roles of anthropologists analyzing these story lines should be to make explicit these stereotypes and the social boundaries they entail, no matter who is offering the story line. Although the analysis may appear initially to undermine positive images for all groups, including the socially and politically subordinate ones, the end goal is to examine all such images as creations which force individuals into undesired roles.

But identity, despite its restricting boundaries, has been part of social negotiations. Civil rights leader James Farmer, in examining the necessity of identity for Blacks, declared that people must have identity before they can renounce it. Farmer, an activist in the 1960s movement in the United States, feels that the Black identity that emerged in the Black Power movement was created to counter the failed thesis of assimilation. Prior to the 1960s, the theory was that if Blacks would cooperate with the system, they would become as White men with invisible black skin, and discrimination would disappear (Farmer 1993). The 1960s demand for a separate Black identity came, in part, as a reaction to unfulfilled promises and to the alienation of having no identity. The Black Power imagery served as a means of combating the dominant Anglo identity.

In this sense, identity is both self-protection weaponry and bargaining chip. No one in control is willing to negotiate sharing power unless the others appear strong enough to take the power. The clash of identities comes in the fear of losing and/or being denied control of society in the social, political, and financial realms.

A focus on bounded identity, especially at sites embodying American creation mythology, will become increasingly important as the demographics of American society shift. This shift is of particular interest to people living on demographic borders, such as San Antonio.[3] This study is a means of analyzing and then negotiating the identities we have created and perpetuated, most particularly in our narratives of the past—histories, reenactments, and "traditional" ceremonies. All who profess the past should apply a critical eye and ear to descriptions of society's origins, and we all must become increasingly aware of subtleties within our story lines in the ways in which we depict others. The point of dissent for women, Hispanics, Blacks, and others depicted as the subordinate in our creation stories is obvious: no one wants to play the subordinate role. No one wants assigned to them "innate" and "inferior" characteristics. These narratives of the past possess in current society (despite our antidiscrimination and desegregation laws) the power to create and enforce a social hierarchy. By analyzing our mythologies, gender dichotomies, and kinship claims we can determine the source of authority in our society, and question its underlying logic.

But in asking that we question authority's base, I am not necessarily advocating the empowerment of one group at the expense of another. I ask instead that we recognize that all identities are weapons in the struggle for power and authority, and as such often intensify anger and serve as barriers to resolving conflict between people. The catastrophic effects of aggressive social identity appear in nationalism, with one group using a claim of ethnic superiority to "cleanse" society of others whom the dominant group declares to be "naturally" inferior.

The first step in resolving conflict between ethnicities comes in rethinking the created divisions between groups, especially in historical narratives. Identity is an external image projected against others; it is *not* an innate quality. Examining the roles we assign one another in our sacred narratives allows us to view the hierarchical construction of these roles and to question their "naturalness." We must delve into the implicit social hierarchy of "the past" as offered in these narratives to allow a more equitable present.

# Notes

## Introduction

1. Throughout this work I use the term *Hispanic* as do the people of San Antonio to distinguish themselves and/or others as people related in some way to Mexico, Spain, Cuba, or another country with Spanish as the primary language. People employing this term juxtapose *Hispanic* to *Anglo*. People who appear as the Anglo side of this created dichotomy do not usually refer to themselves publicly as such, whereas many of the people who appear as part of the Hispanic side openly declare themselves as Hispanic. *Anglo*, then, is often a term used by Hispanics for the Other in an emotionally charged sense.

2. See Richard Slotkin's *Regeneration through Violence: The Mythology of the American Frontier, 1600–1860* regarding the origins of this frontier mythology.

## Chapter 1. Ancestors and Descendants

1. The original site of the mission was across the San Antonio River from Alamo Plaza.

2. The other Spanish missions in the San Antonio area are often called sister missions in relation to the Alamo. The following description of the Mission Trail appears in a brochure produced by the San Antonio Convention and Visitors Bureau: "Now a part of the National Park System it [the Mission Trail] is America's most complete mission complex. The four sister missions of the Alamo each have exciting histories of their own."

3. Montejano uses "Mexican" instead of "Mexican American" or "Hispanic" when denoting ethnicity. Such terminology reflects the political stance of Montejano's history. As the term "Mexicans" for Mexican Americans/Hispanics is often used in a derogatory sense by Anglos, perhaps Montejano and other Hispanics are attempting to replace the stinging effect of the word by using it proudly, much as persons of German ancestry may declare themselves German.

4. Perhaps the domestic-help employment of many Blacks early in San

Antonio's history made proximity to the base and the northside townships important. In this sense, Fort Sam Houston serves as a federal boundary between the two communities.

5. The Greater San Antonio Chamber of Commerce reported in 1989 that over ten million people visited San Antonio in 1988, bringing in about $1.2 billion to the city.

6. Culture with a capital *C* involves the civilization-versus-wilderness distinction; it is cultivated gardens, fine arts, and elegant homes. But culture with a lowercase *c* is ethnicity, which seemingly can be bought and sold at the Mercado in downtown San Antonio.

7. This assignment to the "northwest" distinction may have been made because many tourists are warned about entering the west side of San Antonio.

8. In his study of such North American tourist sites, Umberto Eco describes this hyperreality:

> [F]or historical information to be absorbed, it has to assume the aspect of a reincarnation. To speak of things that one wants to connote as real, these things must seem real. The "completely real" becomes identified with the "completely fake." Absolute unreality is offered as real presence. . . . The sign aims to be the thing, to abolish the distinction of the reference, the mechanism of replacement. Not the image of the thing, but its plaster cast. Its double in other words.

> (Eco 1986:7)

9. Until 1992, the Alamo scenes were the ultimate ones viewed by visitors to the museum. The museum manager has since moved the Alamo defenders to the next-to-last exhibit. The Alamo heroes have been replaced in this grand finale role by none other than Jesus Christ, who is depicted going through his sacrifice: in the Garden of Gethsemane, carrying the cross, crucified, and finally resurrected.

### Chapter 2. Fiesta Heirs

1. Unless a reference appears after information on the history of Fiesta, the historical information was part of an exhibit organized by the Institute of Texan Cultures in San Antonio for the 1991 Fiesta San Antonio centennial.

2. The Battle of Flowers event began as an assemblage of San Antonio's socially elite women, and remains as such today. The current parade features the entire court of the Order of the Alamo, with the newly crowned queen, princess, and duchesses, along with floats representing various groups in the city.

3. In his article about King Antonio, Tom Walker notes this pride of LULAC members for their Rey Feo:

Members of LULAC don't mind telling you that their king is a more serious king (he raises money for those scholarships), more of a people's
king (he is chosen by the community, not a club), a more active king
year-round (he is the guest of honor during non-Fiesta months at fetes in
Corpus Christi, Austin, Brownsville, and Laredo), and even a more "vi-
sual" king, than Antonio is.

(Walker 1983:218–219)


## Chapter 3. Texas in Her Birth

1. The DRT found this poem so important that it not only asked a member of the Children of the Republic of Texas to recite it at the memorial
service; it also printed the entire poem in the program for the 1990 service.

2. I am indebted to Jim Steely of the Texas Historical Commission for
pointing out this importance of "manifest destiny" in the distinction
"defenders."

3. Perry McWilliams, in his article "The Alamo Story: From Fact to
Fable," suggests that the line crossing is similar to the Last Supper:

According to Biblical tradition, Jesus declares during the meal that his
death is to be a sacrifice for the benefit of others rather than a simple act
of criminal crucifixion. In the same way, the speech and line-crossing in-
cidents perform the function of a vow to die sacrificial deaths so that
fellow Texans will be spared.

(McWilliams 1978:229)


4. This cowardice is echoed in the other character associated with the
Napoleonic past: Louis (Moses) Rose. In the mythology, he is the only man
who will not cross Travis's line; he deserts the Alamo under cover of night
and in the defenders' darkening hour.

5. Crockett is the spirit within the Alamo trinity, and as such, he is
immortal and has a tendency to resurface in various places after the Battle
of the Alamo.

6. In the Battle of Thermopylae, a small band of Spartans under the leadership of Leonidas defended a pass through mountains against a superior
Persian force led by Xerxes. For several days the Spartans held off the Per-
sians until a Malisian told Xerxes of a path over the mountain to Thermopylae. Once Leonidas realized that he had been outmaneuvered by the Per-
sians, he made the decision to stay and die at the pass, but he excused two
of his men from battle as they had "pain with their eyes" and sent them out
as messengers (Herodotus 1987:546–552).

7. This interpretation works well if we ignore Moses Rose and his departure from the garrison before the battle; however, the story of Rose's escape
did not surface until well after the saying had become popular.

8. In his book *Duel of Eagles: The Mexican and U.S. Fight for the Alamo*, Jeff Long writes:

> The Bowie fairy tale states that [Bowie] and Ursula had two cherished children, both of whom succumbed to the [cholera] plague. According to stock legend, the grief-stricken husband fell into desperate alcoholism and never fully revived until the Texas Revolution. In fact, there were no Bowie children.
>
> (Long 1990:32)

Even though the flesh-and-blood James Bowie had no children, the Bowie of the Texas creation mythology must appear as a father figure whose potential for family has come and gone.

9. Sylvia Grider notes that the often-cited service of Rose under Napoleon foreshadows Santa Anna's appeal to Sam Houston's pride in fate allowing Houston to capture the "Napoleon of the West" (Grider 1989).

10. The primary code of this new order is honor, which historian Bertram Wyatt-Brown proclaims as "the keystone of the slaveholding South's morality" (Wyatt-Brown 1982:vii). If Travis's refusals to surrender or retreat ring with a moral tone, it is because protecting one's personal honor was recognized in Travis's homeland as the "superior moral force" within southern society. As Wyatt-Brown notes, the gossips at the tavern exercised more influence than did the frowning deacons (Wyatt-Brown 1982:xvii–xviii).

11. Richard Slotkin explains that the image of the mediating hero evolves in American mythology through acculturation of the Europeans in America:

> If the first American mythology portrayed the colonist as a captive or a destroyer of Indians, the subsequent acculturated versions of the myth showed him growing closer to the Indian and the wild land. New versions of the hero emerged, characters whose role was that of mediating between civilization and savagery, white and red.
>
> (Slotkin 1973:21)

12. According to a state employee at the information desk of the Texas State Capitol, the Twin Sisters are "buried" near Houston. They were placed in the ground during the Civil War so that they would not fall into the hands (or arms) of Union soldiers (personal communication: 1991).

13. Consider images in songs and novels in which women appear as "Daddy's prized possession" with ardent suitors hoping to become the new caretaker of this prize.

### Chapter 4. Ethnic Eves and Anglo Marys

1. I derive my opposition between nature and culture in the mythology from Claude Lévi-Strauss's structural analysis of myth in which nature is

the "raw," or unrefined, state of human life and culture is the "cooked," or refined, state (cf. Lévi-Strauss 1969). In my use of this dichotomy, "nature" incorporates three of its various meanings as employed by Maurice and Jean Bloch in their historical analysis of the term: nature is simultaneously (1) a "chronologically pre-social state," (2) the "internal processes of the human body, especially instincts and emotions but also reproductive processes," and (3) the "way of life of primitive peoples whether real, imaginary or a mixture of the two" (Bloch and Bloch 1980:27–28).

2. Texas' independence marked the beginning of the loss of northern Mexico that is now the American Southwest.

3. The implied sterility of the union between Santa Anna and Emily Morgan may also stem from their in-between status. Emily as a mulatto and Santa Anna as a Mexican (supposedly a cross between Spanish and Indian) may mythologically have imposed upon them the sterility of a mule.

4. Accounts vary from thirty to two hundred yards in the closeness to which the Texans come before being noticed. George McAlister chooses thirty yards, making the Mexican army seem extraordinarily incompetent.

5. The Rosita character may well be George McAlister's way of slipping his version of Melchora into this film which is supposed to be based on history. McAlister served as executive producer on the film.

6. In the scene protested, the Tennessean is merely trying to get a kiss; it is not, at least not explicitly, as sexual as Leo Garza insinuates. However, it is still a potentially sexual relationship between an Anglo male and a Hispanic female.

7. Heroic characters in the Texas creation mythology seem to walk the line between excessive culture and unrefined nature. In his study of mythology surrounding the westward movement by the United States, Richard Slotkin traces the origin of this aspect of American mythology from its Puritan roots. He finds John Bunyan's *Pilgrim's Progress* the closest model of the heroic quest undertaken by the Puritans: the pilgrim leaves the City of Destruction to journey to the Heavenly City. Slotkin notes the two extremes of the nature/culture dichotomy, both of which were undesirable:

The Indians were emblems of external temptation to sin or of the human mind's dark impulses to sin. England was often portrayed in terms of the City of Destruction—a place from which the righteous must, at all costs, flee.

(Slotkin 1973:39–40)

In the mythology, neither of these extremes is acceptable. The sin of nature and the destruction of overcultivation must be avoided if the Heavenly City—in this case, Texas—is to become a reality.

8. This nineteenth-century view of the proper woman as a sexually anesthetized being reveals the shifting inherent in categories. The asexuality allotted women inverts the placement of women in the nature category based on possession of a womb and breasts. Reproduction, when juxtaposed

to production, is supposedly a more natural process. But women, at least socially proper women, do not seek the sexual experience necessary for reproduction; rather, they simply endure the act for the sake of their husbands.

9. As Paul Ricoeur so aptly asks, "Is it not part of the plot to include the death of each hero in a story that surpasses every individual fate?" (Ricoeur 1980:188).

## Chapter 5. Heroic Kings and Wealthy Queens

1. This description of Texas comes from the sculptor of the cenotaph on Alamo Plaza, Pompeo Coppini, who described his creation of Texas' image thus:

> I endeavored to make it a figure of a majestic matron, strong in body as in character, expressing determination, power, courage, dignity; capable of charity and justice, or restraint and super-intellectuality. . . . She is the Queen of Plenty, the Mother of Heroes, and one of the strongest vertebraes in the backbone of the greatest nation on earth.
>
> (Coppini 1940)

This birth of Texas is made possible, according to the mythology, by the death of the Alamo defenders. Thus, in the ideology it appears fitting to have the figure of Texas on a cenotaph which celebrates new life from the death of heroes. The cenotaph on Alamo Plaza is the inverse of a gravestone, celebrating immortality rather than human remains.

2. In addition to the queen and princess, there are twenty-four duchesses—twelve in-town duchesses and twelve out-of-town duchesses. The appearance in 1989 of H. Ross Perot's daughter Caroline Margot Perot as one of the out-of-town duchesses reveals the type of women invited to participate in the Order of the Alamo coronation.

3. For this popularity rating, I am relying on the results of the survey conducted September 1990 through August 1991 by the Texas Department of Transportation. Among the short-term visitors within the United States (the largest group responding to the questionnaire), the Alamo was the number one attraction and the San Antonio River Walk was second in the entire state of Texas. Among visitors from outside of the United States, the Alamo was first and the San Antonio River Walk was fourth.

4. I am indebted to anthropologist Michaele Haynes, who accompanied me to the investiture of King Antonio, for pointing out this activity. From our "seats" on the curb to the right of the grandstands, we watched as people exchanged pins denoting their particular group and the Fiesta event it sponsored.

5. Sociologist Georg Simmel notes that secrecy offers "the possibility of a second world alongside the manifest world" (Simmel 1950:330). The Texas Cavaliers affect a knowledge of this inner world in their enclosure within the shrine during the sunset hour.

6. The Menger Hotel remains an important site for presenting San Antonio society women, such as the Queen of the Order of the Alamo.

7. The mayor's comment is indicative of the nature/culture comparison between business cities of the East and San Antonio which, at this point, is situated on the border with wild, undeveloped West Texas.

8. The popular 1962 song "The Man Who Shot Liberty Valance" by Burt Bacharach and Hal David describes the hero as a "stranger" who will bring order to a "troubled land." Travis is the same image of a stranger from the East carrying the law of civilization with him to this western wilderness.

9. After the 1991 coronation, one father walked over to the moving van onto which his daughter was loaded (moving vans are the only means of transporting the women in their massive coronation gowns) and called out to her, "Good work, Honey!"

### Chapter 6. Matronly Daughters

1. There is a small crossover in the DRT and BOFA membership rolls, but not on the same scale as the crossover between the Texas Cavaliers and the Order of the Alamo rolls.

2. Capitalism receives a slap here, primarily because the DRT seeks to become the guardian who preserves the Alamo, which the Daughters proclaim a shrine, from outside aggression. They are the women protecting the private, sacred space from the commercial world. But a secondary reason may be tied to the origin of this "commercial greed": the prospective buyer was an "Eastern syndicate."

3. In her disappearing heroine status, De Zavala is similar to another Hispanic figure, Juan Seguín, who initially aids the Texans in their fight for independence from Mexico. His name is often dropped from the histories after the Texas Revolution because he becomes more and more disillusioned in the Texans' struggle with and distrust of Mexico.

4. The DRT finds it ironic that progress could destroy the Alamo because the creation myth has progress creating Texas out of chaotic wilderness.

5. At this time (1994) I have been unable to discover what De Zavala meant by "the main building," or whether or not the plaque is still on the wall, hidden by plaster.

6. These photographs bearing De Zavala's inscriptions are in the Adina De Zavala personal papers file at the Barker Library in Austin, Texas.

7. The Anglo/Hispanic division is not an absolute one, as is apparent in Anglo Frank Tolbert's writing about De Zavala first.

### Chapter 7. Adopted Daughter

1. The Alamo Rangers are specially trained guards who protect both the inside and the outside of the state property. According to one San Antonio Living Historian Association member, the Alamo Rangers received an upgrade in their ammunition during Operation Desert Shield/Storm of 1990/1991, replacing the relatively harmless shot that would sting but not kill a

person with lethal bullets. One employee of the Texas Historical Commission claims that the Alamo Rangers never had any type of gun until very recently. One security official at the Alamo claimed that the Alamo Rangers have been armed since 1983 or 1984, and that there has been no upgrade in their ammunition.

2. According to a Trinity University student working in the gift shop, the biggest sellers were the coonskin hats, followed by books. She explained that two of the largest sales days were "Baptist Tuesday and Wednesday," when the annual convention of Southern Baptists was taking place in San Antonio (Amy Plogg 1989).

3. The Alamo Rangers unit is almost exclusively male, but there has been at least one female within the group. However, the image of the group is that of the protective male guarding the matronly Daughters within.

4. Ironically, the space in which these gardens sit would have been "watered" by the blood of Mexican soldiers attacking the compound.

5. The popular version of "The Yellow Rose of Texas" changes the first line of the chorus from "She's the sweetest rose of color this darkie ever knew" to "She's the sweetest little rosebud that Texas ever knew." In upholding the Texas creation ideology, the Black blood which gives the rose its hue must be acknowledged less publicly on the midnight plain of the San Jacinto Memorial or inside a hotel lobby; it must not appear in front of the shrine itself.

6. Such a description would also exclude the Europeans, though their names do not appear in the marked contrast that the Hispanic names do within the roll call.

7. The Alamo door guard at the 1990 Memorial Service informed me that the service was full and therefore not open to the public, but when I explained my interest in studying the Alamo, he obtained permission for me to be admitted.

8. During the protest, a tourist requested permission to have his picture taken standing next to the Alamo facade, and he was allowed to go onto state property.

## Chapter 8. Rejected Suitors

1. One problem with this statement by John Leal is that the ancestors of the DRT have almost certainly paid taxes as well, making them owners in the same right.

2. The cartoon tabloid to which Garcia refers was produced by the Magnolia Petroleum Company (which later became part of Socony-Mobil Oil Company, Inc.) from the late 1920s through the late 1950s under the title *Texas History Movies*. According to George Ward of the Texas State Historical Association, publication stopped after objections surfaced during the late 1950s that some of the drawings and dialogues were demeaning to Indians, Mexicans, and Blacks. A collection of the cartoons, with the most offensive comics deleted, was rereleased in 1974 by the Texas State Histori-

cal Association, which had obtained the copyright for the cartoons (Ward 1974).

3. The Rey Feo controversy in 1989 involved a question of whether some of the funds raised for the LULAC scholarships were used to pay for a deficit associated with the Fiesta Flambeau Rey Feo parade. The controversy pitted the local LULAC Council No. 2 against the national LULAC organization, with Rey Feo Nick Garza defying orders from the LULAC president Jose Garcia de Lara.

4. Visitors to the Alamo normally are required to use the side exit from the building, which leaves the visitors facing the gift shop entrance. Only special guests, such as Queen Elizabeth II and the Texas Cavaliers, may exit the building from the front doors.

**Chapter 9. Heroes in the Street**

1. In the 1989 presentation of This Hallowed Ground, Alamo Plaza, the salute was only to the Alamo defenders. The Mexican soldiers did not receive such a salute during the 1989 performance.

**Conclusion. The Responsible Anthropologist**

1. The problem with this theory is that at least three other Jewish Alamo defenders, Avram (Anthony) Wolf and his two sons, died in the 1836 battle. Why were they not encouraged to leave as well?

2. Such "unfortunate" castings are not uncommon in historical pageantry. David Glassberg notes that in the 1909 New York City Hudson-Fulton Celebration, Black children played the role of Native Americans (Glassberg 1990: 114).

3. The front page of the *San Antonio Express-News*, September 29, 1993, offered a report of the growing Hispanic presence, and the report contained the prediction that by the year 2050, Hispanics will be the "largest minority group" in the United States. The report also predicted that the Anglo population of 2050 will account for only 52.5 percent of the population, down 21.1 percentage points for the Anglo population predicted for 1995 (73.6 percent of the population).

# Bibliography

Ables, L. Robert
 1967. "The Second Battle for the Alamo." *Southwestern Historical Quarterly* 70, no. 3: 372–413.
Abrahams, Roger, and Richard Bauman, eds.
 1981. *"And Other Neighborly Names": Social Process and Cultural Image in Texas Folklore.* Austin: University of Texas Press.
Arnold, Charles August
 1928. "The Folk-lore, Manners, and Customs of the Mexicans in San Antonio, Texas." Master's thesis, University of Texas.
Austin, Mrs. Stephen F.
 1936. *The Alamo: The Cradle of Texas Liberty.* San Antonio: International Printing Co.
Ayers, Edward L.
 1984. *Vengeance and Justice: Crime and Punishment in the 19th-Century American South.* New York: Oxford University Press.
Banks, C. Stanley
 1952. "The Alamo, Shrine of Texas Liberty." *American Heritage*, fall, 40–43.
Barker-Benfield, Ben
 1974. "The Spermatic Economy: A Nineteenth-Century View of Sexuality." *Feminist Studies* 1: 45–74.
Baylis, Thomas
 1983. "Leadership Change in Contemporary San Antonio." In *The Politics of San Antonio: Community, Progress, and Power*, edited by David R. Johnson, John A. Booth, and Richard J. Harris, 95–113. Lincoln: University of Nebraska Press.
Black, Max
 1981. "Metaphor." In *Philosophical Perspectives on Metaphor*, edited by Mark Johnson, 63–82. Minneapolis: University of Minnesota Press.
Blackwelder, Julia Kirk
 1984. *Women of the Depression: Caste and Culture in San Antonio, 1929–1939.* College Station: Texas A&M University Press.

Bloch, Maurice, and Jean Helen Bloch
1980. "Women and the Dialectics of Nature in Eighteenth-Century French Thought." In *Nature, Culture, and Gender*, edited by Carol P. MacCormack and Marilyn Strathern, 25–41. New York: Cambridge University Press.

Booth, John A., and David R. Johnson
1983. "Community, Progress, and Power in San Antonio." In Johnson, Booth, and Harris, eds., *The Politics of San Antonio*, vii–xii. Lincoln: University of Nebraska Press.

Brischetto, Robert, Charles L. Cotrell, and R. Michael Stevens
1983. "Conflict and Change in the Political Culture of San Antonio in the 1970s." In Johnson, Booth, and Harris, eds., *The Politics of San Antonio*, 75–94. Lincoln: University of Nebraska Press.

Broussard, Ray F.
1967. *San Antonio during the Texas Republic: A City in Transition*. El Paso: Texas Western Press.

Buckley, Richard
1911. "A Tale of the Alamo." Reprinted in *San Antonio Legacy* (1979), edited by Donald Everett, 87–96. San Antonio: Trinity University Press.

Bunkley, Anita
1989. *Emily, The Yellow Rose: A Texas Legend*. Houston: Rinard Publishing.

Butterfield, Jack
1960. *Women of the Alamo*. San Antonio: Daughters of the Republic of Texas.
1961. *Clara Driscoll Rescued the Alamo*. San Antonio: The Library Committee, DRT.

Carrol, Bess
1936. "Heroes of Alamo Elect to Die." *San Antonio Light*, March 3.

Chabot, Frederick C.
1935. *The Alamo; Mission, Fortress, and Shrine*. San Antonio: The Leake Co.

Clendenin, Lucile
1932. "The Savior of the Alamo." *Texas Commercial News*, January.

Colquitt, Gov. O. B.
1913. *Message of Governor O. B. Colquitt to the Thirty-third Legislature Relating to the Alamo Property*. Austin: Von Boeckmann–Jones Co.

Coppini, Pompeo
1940. "The Alamo Cenotaph." Comments from a radio talk on station KTSA in San Antonio.

Cox, Waynne
1990. Interview in San Antonio.

Crimmins, Col. M. L.
1946. "The Storming of San Antonio de Bexar in 1835." *West Texas Historical Association Year Book* 22, October.

Curtis, Albert
1961. *Remember the Alamo Heroes*. San Antonio: The Clegg Company.

Daffan, Katie
    1908. *Texas Hero Stories: An Historical Reader for the Grades.* Boston: Benjamin H. Sanborn & Co.
Daughters of the Republic of Texas (DRT)
    1892. Constitution and By-Laws of the Daughters of the Republic of Texas.
    1893. Proceedings from the Second Annual Meeting of the Daughters of the Republic of Texas.
    1901. Program for the Celebration of San Jacinto Day, April 21, 1901, by the Schools of Texas.
    1990a. Information packet compiled for schoolteachers.
    1990b. Letter sent to Curtis Tunnell, Executive Director of the Texas Historical Commission.
de la Teja, Jesus F., and John Wheat
    1985. "Bexar: Profile of a Tejano Community, 1820–1832." *Southwestern Historical Quarterly* 89, no. 1: 7–34.
Dobie, J. Frank
    1939. *In the Shadow of History.* Austin: Texas Folklore Society.
    1953. *Stories of Christmas and the Bowie Knife.* Austin: The Steck Company.
    1959. "No Help for the Alamo." *True West,* May–June.
Dundes, Alan
    1980. *Interpreting Folklore.* Bloomington: Indiana University Press.
Dyer, Robert
    1986. "Church of Destiny." *True West,* March.
Eaton, Jack
    1980. *Excavations at the Alamo Shrine.* Special report no. 10. Center for Archaeological Research at the University of Texas at San Antonio.
Eco, Umberto
    1986. *Travels in Hyperreality,* translated by William Weaver. San Diego: Harcourt Brace Jovanovich.
Esparza, Reynaldo
    1988. Interview in San Antonio.
Everett, Donald
    1961. "San Antonio Welcomes the 'Sunset'—1877." *Southwestern Historical Quarterly* 65, no. 1: 46–60.
Farmer, James
    1993. Interview in Fredericksburg, Virginia.
"Fight for Queen of the Alamo"
    1905. Barker Library files in Austin, Texas.
Ford, John S.
    1895. *Origin and Fall of the Alamo.* San Antonio: Johnson Brothers Printing Co.
Foster, Nancy H., and Ben Fairbank, Jr.
    1989. *The Texas Monthly Guide to San Antonio.* Revised, 3d ed. Houston: Lone Star Books.
Fox, Anne
    1990. Interview in San Antonio.

Fox, Anne, Feris A. Bass, Jr., and Thomas R. Hester

1976. *The Archaeology and History of Alamo Plaza*. Archaeology report no. 16. Center for Archaeological Research at the University of Texas at San Antonio.

Garcia, Nef

1989. Interview in San Antonio.

Gibson, Tucker

1983. "Mayoralty Politics in San Antonio, 1955–79." In Johnson, Booth, and Harris, eds., *The Politics of San Antonio*, 114–129. Lincoln: University of Nebraska Press.

Glassberg, David

1990. *American Historical Pageantry: The Uses of Tradition in the Early Twentieth Century*. Chapel Hill: University of North Carolina Press.

*Good Roads*

1914. "Battle of the Alamo." Texas Field and National Guardsman. San Antonio: Guessaz & Ferlet Co., 3–11.

Gould, Stephen

1883. *The Alamo City Guide*. New York: Macgowen & Slipper.

Graham, Henry

1976. *History of the Texas Cavaliers*.

Greater San Antonio Chamber of Commerce

1990. *Annual Report of Economic Indicators*.

Greer, John

1967. *The Stratigraphy, Features, and Artifacts*. Produced by the State Building Commission. Vol. 3 in a series on an archaeological investigation at Mission San Antonio de Valero (the Alamo).

Grider, Sylvia

1989. "The Function of Texas Historical Legends." Paper delivered at the Ninth International Folk Narrative Congress in Budapest, Hungary.

Grimes, Ronald L.

1976. *Symbol and Conquest: Public Ritual and Drama in Santa Fe, New Mexico*. Ithaca: Cornell University Press.

Guerra, Henry

1988. Interview in San Antonio.

1990a. Letter to Curtis Tunnell.

1990b. Comments during a radio interview of Jeff Long by Alan Dale on station WOAI in San Antonio.

Habig, Marion A., O.F.M.

1977. *The Alamo Mission: San Antonio de Valero, 1718–1793*. Chicago: Franciscan Herald Press.

Hall-Quest, Olga W.

1948. *Shrine of Liberty: The Alamo*. New York: E. P. Dutton & Co.

Handler, Richard

1985. "On Dialogue and Destructive Analysis: Problems in Narrating Nationalism and Ethnicity." *Journal of Anthropological Research* 41: 171–182.

1988. "The Center in American Culture: Analysis and Critique." *Anthropological Quarterly* 61, no. 1: 1–2.

Handler, Richard, and William Saxton
1988. "Dyssimulation: Reflexivity, Narrative, and the Quest for Authenticity in 'Living History.'" *Current Anthropology* 3: 242–260.

Haynes, Michaele
1991. Numerous conversations in person and over the telephone during and after Fiesta 1991.
1992. Telephone interview.

Hearon, Shelby
1986. "The Guardian." *Texas Monthly*, January, 166.

Henson, Margaret
1986. "She's the Real Thing." *Texas Highways* 33, no. 4 (April): 61.
1990. Telephone interview.

Herodotus
1987. *The History*. Translated by David Grene. Chicago: University of Chicago Press.

Highwater, Jamake
1990. *Myth and Sexuality*. New York: Meridian.

Hinojosa, Gilbert
1988. Interview in San Antonio.
1990. Interview in San Antonio.

Hobsbawm, Eric J., and Terence O. Ranger, eds.
1983. *The Invention of Tradition*. New York: Cambridge University Press.

Humble Oil Company
1936. *Twice-Told Tales of Texas*. Houston: Humble Oil Co.

Hutton, Paul A.
1985. Introduction to Susan Schoelwer's *Alamo Images: Changing Perceptions of a Texas Experience*, 3–17. Dallas: DeGolyer Library and Southern Methodist University Press.
1986. "A Tale of Two Alamos." *SMU Mustang*, spring.

Jacobs, Bonnie Sue
1989. "Page's Fiesta Ties Span Generations." *North San Antonio Times*, April, 3.

Jakes, John
1986. *Susanna of the Alamo: A True Story*. San Diego: Harcourt Brace Jovanovich.

Janacek, Balthazar
1991. Telephone interview.

Johnson, David R., John A. Booth, and Richard J. Harris, eds.
1983. *The Politics of San Antonio: Community, Progress, and Power*. Lincoln: University of Nebraska Press.

Jones, Richard
1983. "San Antonio's Spatial Economic Structure, 1955–80." In *The Politics of San Antonio: Community, Progress, and Power*, edited by David R.

Johnson, John A. Booth, and Richard J. Harris, 28–52. Lincoln: University of Nebraska Press.

Jordan, Terry
1986. "A Century and a Half of Ethnic Change in Texas, 1836–1986." *Southwestern Historical Quarterly* 89, no. 2: 385–442.

Katz, Harvey
1972. *Shadow on the Alamo: New Heroes Fight Old Corruption in Texas Politics.* Garden City, N.Y.: Doubleday & Company, Inc.

Kelley, Mike
1990. "Edited for Length: Alamo Cut from Epic to Mini-Miniseries." *Austin American-Statesman.*

Kilgore, Dan
1978. *How Did Davy Die?* College Station: Texas A&M University Press.

King, C. Richard
1976. *Susanna Dickinson: Messenger of the Alamo.* Austin: Shoal Creek Publishers.

Kurin, Richard
1993. Discussion of papers presented at the annual American Anthropology Association meeting in Washington, D.C.

Lack, Paul D.
1992. *The Texas Revolutionary Experience: A Political and Social History, 1835–1836.* College Station: Texas A&M University Press.

Leal, John
1988. Interview in San Antonio.
1990. Personal letter.

Lévi-Strauss, Claude
1963. *Structural Anthropology.* New York: Basic Books.
1969. *The Raw and the Cooked.* New York: Harper and Row.
1978. *Myth and Meaning.* Toronto: University of Toronto Press.

Lindsay, Diana
1990. "A Brief Alamo History." In Daughters of the Republic of Texas information packet for schoolteachers.

Linenthal, Edward Tabor
1991. *Sacred Ground: Americans and Their Battlefields.* Urbana: University of Illinois Press.

Long, Jeff
1990. *Duel of Eagles: The Mexican and U.S. Fight for the Alamo.* New York: William Morrow and Company, Inc.

Looscan, Adele B.
1904. "The Work of the Daughters of the Republic of Texas in Behalf of the Alamo." *Texas Historical Association Quarterly* 8, no. 1: 79–82.

Lord, Walter
1961. *A Time to Stand.* New York: Harper and Brothers.

Lowman, Shepard C.
1942. "The Siege and Fall of the Alamo." The James Monroe Hill Texas History Essay Award in the High Schools of Texas, offered by the Sons of the Republic of Texas.

Maguire, Jack
   1990. *A Century of Fiesta in San Antonio.* Austin: Eakin Press.
Maverick, Mary A.
   1889. *The Fall of the Alamo.*
McAlister, George A.
   1988a. *Alamo . . . The Price of Freedom: A History of Texas.* San Antonio: Docutex, Inc.
   1988b. *A Time to Love . . . A Time to Die: A Tale of the Men Who Forged the Republic of Texas—Their Lives and Loves.* San Antonio: Docutex, Inc.
McCain, Johnny M.
   1981. "Texas and the Mexican Labor Question, 1942–1947." *Southwestern Historical Quarterly* 85, no. 1: 43–64.
McCaleb, Walter F.
   1956. *The Alamo.* San Antonio: The Naylor Co.
McDonald, Archie P.
   1976. *Travis.* Austin: The Pemberton Press.
McWilliams, Perry
   1978. "The Alamo Story: From Fact to Fable." *Journal of the Folklore Institute* 15, no. 3: 221–233.
Melendrez, Sonny
   1991. Interview in San Antonio.
Moffitt, Virginia M.
   1953. *Remember the Alamo!* Dallas: Upshaw.
Montejano, David
   1987. *Anglos and Mexicans in the Making of Texas, 1836–1986.* Austin: University of Texas Press.
Muller, Edwin
   1940. "Remember the Alamo." *Reader's Digest,* October, 10–14.
Myers, John M.
   1948. *The Alamo.* New York: E. P. Dutton and Co., Inc.
Nackman, Mark E.
   1975. *A Nation within a Nation: The Rise of Texas Nationalism.* Port Washington, N.Y.: Kennikat Press.
O'Donohoe, Joseph G.
   1936. "Catholics Who Gave Their Lives in the Alamo." *Southern Messenger,* March 5.
Order of the Alamo
   1949. Annual Report.
   1975. *History of the Order of the Alamo, 1960–1975.* Vol. 4.
   1976. Annual Report.
Ornish, Natalie
   1991. *Pioneer Jewish Texans: Their Impact on Texas and American History for Four Hundred Years, 1590–1990.* Dallas: Texas Heritage Press.
Pearson, Jim, Ben Proctor, and William Conroy
   1987. *Texas: The Land and Its People.* Hendrick Long Publisher.

Pennybaker, Anna J. H.
1907. *A History of Texas for Schools*. Rev. ed. Austin: Mrs. Percy V. Pennybaker.

Pisano, Marina
1978. "The Kingdom Crowns Its Queen." *San Antonio, the Magazine of San Antonio*, April, 42–50.

Plogg, Amy
1989. Interview in San Antonio.

Potter, Reuben M.
1878. "The Fall of the Alamo." *Magazine of American History* 2, no. 1 (January): 1–21.

Proctor, Ben
1986. *The Battle of the Alamo*. Austin: Texas State Historical Association.

Pugh, Clifford
1986. "The Alamo: The 13 Days That Shaped Texas History." *Houston Post*, February 23.

Rappaport, Roy A.
1993. "The Anthropology of Trouble." Distinguished Lecture in General Anthropology. *American Anthropologist* 95, no. 2: 295–303.

Ray, Fredric
1955. *The Story of the Alamo*. San Antonio.

Rebel, Hermann
1989. "Cultural Hegemony and Class Experience: A Critical Reading of Recent Ethnological-Historical Approaches," parts 1 and 2. *American Ethnologist* 16, nos. 1 and 2: 117–136, 350–365.

"Remember the Alamo"
1987. *Parade Magazine*, July 12.

Ricoeur, Paul
1965. *History and Truth*. Translated by Charles A. Kebley. Evanston, Ill.: Northwestern University Press.
1977. *Rule of Metaphor*. Translated by Robert Czerny, with Kathleen McLaughlin and John Costello. Toronto: University of Toronto Press.
1980. "Narrative Time." *Critical Inquiry* 7, no. 1: 169–191.

Roberts, Oran M.
1881. *A Description of Texas: Its Advantages and Resources*. St. Louis: Gilbert Books.

Rosenbaum, Robert J.
1981. *Mexicano Resistance in the Southwest: "The Sacred Right of Self-Preservation."* Austin: University of Texas Press.

Sahlins, Marshall
1985. *Islands of History*. Chicago: University of Chicago Press.

Schmidt, Eric Von
1986. "The Alamo Remembered—from a Painter's Point of View." *Smithsonian* 16, no. 12 (March): 54–67.

Schoelwer, Susan Prendergast
1985. *Alamo Images: Changing Perceptions of a Texas Experience*. Dallas: DeGolyer Library and Southern Methodist University Press.

Sears, John F.
1989. *Sacred Places: American Tourist Attractions in the Nineteenth Century.* New York: Oxford University Press.
Servin, Manuel
1973. "California's Hispanic Heritage: A View into the Spanish Myth." In *New Spain's Far Northern Frontier* (1979), edited by David Weber, 117–134. Albuquerque: University of New Mexico Press.
Shuffler, R. Henderson
1972. "San Jacinto as She Was: Or, What Really Happened on the Plain of St. Hyacinth on a Hot April Afternoon in 1836." In *Observations and Reflections on Texas Folklore*, edited by Francis E. Abernethy, 121–130. Austin: The Encino Press.
Simmel, Georg
1950. *The Sociology of Georg Simmel.* Translated and edited by Kurt H. Wolff. New York: The Free Press.
Skerry, Peter
1993. *Mexican Americans: The Ambivalent Minority.* New York: The Free Press.
Slotkin, Richard
1973. *Regeneration through Violence: The Mythology of the American Frontier, 1600–1860.* Middletown, Conn.: Wesleyan University Press.
Smith, Rebecca W.
1924. *Following the Lone Star: A Pageant of Texas Independence.* Fort Worth: Texas Christian University.
Southerland, John
1936. *The Fall of the Alamo.* San Antonio: The Naylor Company.
Steely, James W.
1990. "Who Really 'Saved' the Alamo?" *Medallion*, March, 5. Austin: Texas Historical Commission.
1991. "Adina De Zavala: Preservationist Extraordinaire." *Medallion*, March, 5. Austin: Texas Historical Commission.
Taylor, Henry Ryder
1936. *History of the Alamo and of the Local Franciscan Missions.* San Antonio: Nic Tengg, Inc.
Tejeda, Juan
1988. Interview in San Antonio.
Tinkle, Lon
1958. *13 Days to Glory.* New York: McGraw-Hill.
Titherington, Richard H.
1874. "The Defenders of the Alamo."
Tjarks, Alicia
1974. "Comparative Demographic Analysis of Texas, 1777–1793." *Southwestern Historical Quarterly* 77, no. 3: 291–338.
Tolbert, Frank
1959. *The Day of San Jacinto.* New York: McGraw-Hill Book Company, Inc.

1961a. "Lone Woman Defended Alamo in Battle of '05." *Dallas News*, February 12.

1961b. "About Great Lady Who Owned Alamo." *Dallas News*, May 29.

Tunnell, Curtis

1990. Interview in Austin.

Turner, Martha Anne

1981. "Emily Morgan: Yellow Rose of Texas." In *Legendary Ladies of Texas*, edited by Francis E. Abernethy, 21–29. Dallas: E-Heart Press.

Wagner, Roy

1975. *Invention of Culture*. Chicago: University of Chicago Press.

Walker, Kenneth

1965. "The Pecan Shellers of San Antonio and Mechanization." *Southwestern Historical Quarterly* 69, no. 1: 44–58.

Walker, Tom

1983. "Hail to Thee, George E. Fischer." *Texas Monthly*, April.

Ward, George B.

1974. Introduction to *Texas History Movies*. Texas State Historical Association and Texas Educational Association.

Warren, Robert Penn

1958a. "Remember the Alamo." *Holiday*, February.

1958b. "How Texas Won Her Freedom." *Holiday*, March.

Weber, David

1982. *The Mexican Frontier, 1821–1846*. Albuquerque: University of New Mexico Press.

Williams, Amelia

1931. *A Critical Study of the Siege of the Alamo and of the Personnel of Its Defenders*. Ph.D. diss., University of Texas.

Woolford, Bess, and Sam Woolford

1957. *Alamo Survey for the Daughters of the Republic of Texas*. Barker Library files in Austin, Texas.

Wright, Mrs. S. J.

1937. *Our Living Alamo: Mission San Antonio de Valero*. Dallas: Banks Upshaw & Company.

Wyatt-Brown, Bertram

1982. *Southern Honor: Ethics and Behavior in the Old South*. New York: Oxford University Press.

Zavala, Adina De

1911. *The Story of the Siege and Fall of the Alamo. A Resume*. San Antonio.

1917. *History of the Alamo and Other Missions in San Antonio*.

Zelman, Donald

1983. "Alazan-Apache Courts: A New Deal Response to Mexican-American Housing Conditions in San Antonio." *Southwestern Historical Quarterly* 87, no. 2: 122–150.

# Index